Haints

Haints

American Ghosts, Millennial Passions, and
Contemporary Gothic Fictions

ARTHUR REDDING

THE UNIVERSITY OF ALABAMA PRESS
Tuscaloosa

The University of Alabama Press
Tuscaloosa, Alabama 35487-0380
uapress.ua.edu

Hardcover edition published 2011.
Paperback edition published 2019.
eBook edition published 2011.

Inquiries about reproducing material from this work should be addressed to
the University of Alabama Press.

Typeface: Minion Pro

Cover image: © Vitali Dyatchenko | Dreamstime.com
Cover design: Gary Gore

Paperback ISBN: 978-0-8173-5974-4

A previous edition of this book has been catalogued by the Library of
Congress as follows:
Library of Congress Cataloging-in-Publication Data
Redding, Arthur F., 1964–
Haints : American ghosts, millennial passions, and contemporary gothic
fictions / Arthur Redding.
p. cm. — (Introduction: A land without ghosts — Haints and nation: ghosts
and the narrative of national identity — Memory, race, ethnicity, and violence
—Abandoning hope in American fiction: Catalogs of gothic catastrophe —
Conclusion: American innocence.)
Includes bibliographical references and index.
ISBN 978-0-8173-1746-1 (cloth : alk. paper) — ISBN 978-0-8173-8572-9
(electronic)
1. Ghost stories, American—History and criticism. 2. Gothic fiction (Literary
genre), American—History and criticism. 3. Ghosts in literature. 4. Collective
memory in literature. 5. National characteristics, American in literature. I.
Title.
PS374.G45R43   2011
813'.0873309—dc22

2011005992

What ghosts can say—
Even the ghosts of fathers—comes obscurely.
What if the terror stays without the meaning?
—Adrienne Rich, "What Ghosts Can Say"

No justice . . . seems possible or thinkable without the principle of some *responsibility,* beyond all living present, within that which disjoins the living present, before the ghosts of those who are not yet born or who are already dead, be they victims of wars, political or other kinds of violence, nationalist, racist, colonialist, sexist, or other kinds of exterminations, victims of the oppressions of capitalist imperialism or any of the forms of totalitarianism. Without this *non-contemporaneity with itself of the living present,* without that which secretly unhinges it, without this responsibility and this respect for justice concerning those who *are not there,* of those who are no longer or who are not yet *present and living,* what sense would there be to ask the question "where?" "where tomorrow?" "whither?"
—Jacques Derrida, *Specters of Marx*

This book is dedicated to
the memory of Karla Smith.

Contents

Acknowledgments

This work was originally conceived in the mid 1990s, when I found myself in Central Europe teaching a variety of courses on contemporary American literature. My students and I were surprised to encounter so many ghosts in the writing we considered and were spurred to begin a shared inquiry into the presence of ghosts in American novels. My first and most heartfelt thanks is to all of my students—at Masaryk University in Brno, Charles University in Prague, Comenius University in Bratislava, Central European University and Eötvös Lorand University in Budapest, Oklahoma State University, the University of Silesia in Sosnoweic, Poland, and, most recently, at York University in Toronto—for their generosity, patience, enthusiasm, and persistence, as well as for the wealth of their intellectual insight. Over the years and in the various countries, more friends and colleagues than I can mention here have also shared their ears and their ideas. In particular, let me thank Bill Decker and Elizabeth Grubgeld, most stalwart of friends and readers; Tatiani Rapatzikou, collaborator, friend, and mentor; Marcus Grandinetti, whose forays into the field have been inspirational to me and who has pointed me to so many of the critical sources consulted herein; Jared Morrow, who has proven more industrious and able a research assistant than I could possibly have ever hoped for; Dan Waterman, editor-in-chief of the University of Alabama Press, who has been enthusiastic about the project from the start; the anonymous readers at Alabama who have been generous in their appraisals and whip-smart in their criticisms; Joan Redding, for her proofreading and for all other things; and Natallia Barykina, to whom I owe an incalculable debt for her smarts and her patient indulgence and understanding. Publication is supported in part by funds from the Faculty of Liberal Arts and Professional Studies at York University. For this generous assistance, let me thank in particular Associate Dean Barbara Crow. Much of what passes muster herein is due to all of these people and more. Needless to say, all errors and omissions are my own. I should thank as well the staff and colleagues in the Department of English at York University, who have been willing to forgive occasional administrative lapses on my part as I put the finishing touches to this manuscript.

An earlier version of what now constitutes part of the second chapter and a small portion of the introduction was first published as "'Haints': American Ghosts, Ethnic Memory and Contemporary Fiction," in *Mosaic: A Journal for the Interdisciplinary Study of Literature* 34.4 (December 2001): 163–182. A section of chapter 3 was published as "Abandoning Hope in American Fiction of the 1980s: Catalogues of Gothic Catastrophe" in *Gramma* 16 (2008): 273–289. I am grateful to *Mosaic* and to *Gramma* for permission to republish this work.

Other portions of this work have been delivered as presentations at various venues, including the Association for Cultural Studies Crossroads Conference in Kingston, Jamaica, July 2008; the Cultural Studies Colloquium of the University of New Mexico, May 2001; the Conference on Minority Discourses in a Cross-/Transcultural Perspective: Eastern/Central Europe and Canada in Ustron, Poland, April 2002; the Southwest Popular Culture Association Convention in Albuquerque, February 2000; and the April Conference VII at Jagiellonian University in Krakow, March 1996.

Haints

Introduction
A Land Without Ghosts

In 1944, the last year, no doubt, in which it still might have been possible to speak with a straight face of American "innocence," Fei Xiaotang, a Chinese anthropologist and sociologist on a visit to the United States, observed that America is a land without ghosts: "American children hear no stories about ghosts. They spend a dime at the drugstore to buy a Superman comic book. . . . Superman represents actual capabilities or future potential, while ghosts symbolize belief in and reverence for the accumulated past. . . . How could ghosts gain a foothold in American cities? People move about like the tide, unable to form permanent ties with places, still less with other people. . . . In a world without ghosts, life is free and easy. American eyes can gaze straight ahead. But I still think they lack something and I do not envy their life" (qtd. in Arkush and Lee 179–181). By way of opening, I would like to sketch in some aspects of this perceived "lack" in American culture, frame it, perhaps, complicate it, and try to suggest what has driven me to consider it, what makes a dialogue with ghosts, with the "not there," for me, compulsory.

The Southern, African American, and Appalachian colloquialism "haints," from which I draw my title, happily condenses the overlapping domains of my investigation.[1] A *haint* is, first of all, a variant of haunt, a ghost. My subject matter consists primarily of the numerous fictional depictions of the spirit world, depictions that seem omnipresent in American fiction, film, and the culture at large over the last few decades. Many critics have noticed the "haunting" of American culture and have remarked on the topical, but largely unexpected resurgence of the gothic genre of late, citing, in addition to many of the works I consider, new genres from the "New Weird" and Slipstream fictions of the 1990s and after to such phenomenal postmodern successes as Mark Danielewski's much celebrated *House of Leaves* (2000), which Catherine Spooner terms "the quintessential example of contemporary fiction in the Gothic mode" (41). In her survey, *Contemporary Gothic*, which discusses a wide range of phenomena from the music of Siouxsie Sioux and other postpunk "goth" performers (Nick Cave, Marilyn Manson, The Handsome Family) to the notorious but crowd-pleasing *Body Worlds* exhibitions, Spooner highlights the "self-consciousness" and ubiquity of gothic, arguing that is a key feature of "global consumer culture": "Gothic has now become supremely commercialized, be it mainstream or niche-marketed. Gothic no longer crops up only in film and fiction, but also fashion, furniture, computer games, youth culture, advertising. Gothic has always had mass appeal, but in today's economic climate it is big-business. Above all, Gothic sells" (23). Spooner reads contemporary gothic against its apocalyptic grain, understanding it, paradoxically enough, as a form embodying the utopian fantasy of an unbridled market, as "pure commodity, pure luxury, pure excess" (153). Even so, I would venture, it is a form of wish fulfillment undercut with panic, acknowledging, however implicitly, that a limitless market is unsustainable. If contemporary gothic is a genre specific to a hyperaccelerated consumer consciousness, it also partakes, as Anna Sonser reminds us, of market dread: "the essential horror of the gothic is not its goblins and vampires but its latent power to address the disenchanted world of production and the commodification of the social" (12–13).

Citing other popular culture examples from Michael Jackson (whose Gothic freakishness and allure has only been exacerbated by his death) to science fiction, along with writers from Joseph Conrad to Isak Dinesen, Fred Botting, in turn, has catalogued the omnipresence of gothic forms over the course of the twentieth century. Botting accentuates how, especially in "American work, Gothic shadows flicker among representations of cultural, familial and individual fragmentation, in uncanny disruptions of the boundaries between inner being, social values, and concrete reality and in modern forms of barbarism and monstrosity" (156). "In the questioning of narratives of authority and the legitimacy of social forms," he continues, "postmodern Gothic is akin, in its playfulness and duplicity, to the artificialities and ambivalences that surrounded eighteenth century Gothic writing" (157). We might even go so far as to say that the term *gothic* has outpaced *postmodernism* in the contemporary critical vernacular.[2] Accordingly, Allan Lloyd-Smith, in an important essay, "Postmodernism/Gothicism," has indicated the parallels between gothic and postmodern sensibilities and styles. Both genres accentuate indeterminacy, Lloyd-Smith points out, both undermine ontological and epistemological certainties, both are overly indulgent of surface and play on affects, both prefer archaic fantasies to historical rationalism, both can be comic, camp, or burlesque, both are highly reflexive genres, and both not only indulge but positively delight in dread and paranoia.

I will yoke my discussion of contemporary gothic to a consideration of a specifically haunted conception of America at the turn of the millennium. Ever since Leslie Fiedler highlighted the importance of gothic in the American literary tradition in 1960, citing racial and sexual anxiety as a one of the prime "areas of our social life, where nightmare violence and guilt actually exist" (493), critics have argued that gothic permits investigation into realms and themes that are largely muted in conventional channels of discourse or consensual understandings. In her essential work, *Gothic America,* a study to which I am heavily indebted, Teresa A. Goddu further highlights and defends the "generic instability" (5) of the very term *gothic* and suggests that what is most provocative and even productive about gothic is that, as a critical category, it can destabilize "traditional readings of the American literary canon" (8) and, by extension, conventional notions of America itself. Consequently, she links gothic not only to American history, but, paradoxically enough, to that perceived absence of historical sensibility that Fei flags: "the gothic's connection to American history is difficult to identify precisely because of the national and critical myths that America and its literature *have* no history" (9). Indeed, then, it is the nationalist endeavor of literature to evacuate the historical by transforming history into myth that she specifically targets: "the nation's narratives—its foundational fictions and self-mythologizations—are created through a process of displacement: their coherence depends on exclusion" (10). Gothic, ultimately, is a form of writing that conjures up the voices of that which has—and of those who have—been excluded from prevailing representations of America, and "discloses the instability of America's self-representation" (11). Thus, *gothic America:* The incoherence of gothic parallels an incoherent "America," in a rough equation with which I fully concur. Goddu's study covers primarily eighteenth- and nineteenth-century writings; for my part, I wish to extend her critical inquiry into what might be termed a *postnational* or, as I will argue, even a *post-American* condition, when the presumed homogeneity of the national project, as I will elaborate in my first chapter, has been effectively debunked—if not yet fully abandoned.

Recognizing the long legacy of violence in US history and around the globe over the past hundred years or so, this study is also indebted to trauma theory. Collectively, trauma theory refers to an exceptional body of psychoanalytic thinking that has been produced over the past several decades by such critics as Cathy Caruth, Shoshana Felman, Dominick LaCapra, Ruth Leys, and others who have investigated the difficult labor of memory and representation as aftereffects of personal and collective violence, in a world where massive numbers of people have been violently displaced and up-rooted by rampant wars and economic and political catastrophes. Though my purpose in *Haints* is not to pursue in detail the intricacies of these im-pressive critical works, I want to highlight the importance of constructing and elaborating "haunted" narratives—and even fictional narratives—in the aftermath of persistent violence. Traumatic experience introduces a radical and disabling aporia into the conventional narrative mechanism by which human beings stitch together a coherent understanding of the world and our place within it. Often, survivors of extreme violence are blocked in their ef-forts to "move on" and establish functioning lives, which is why testifying to the unspeakable events they have undergone is understood to be crucial for therapeutic as well as for political purposes. Thus, as Linda Belau emphasizes, the Freudian concepts of remembering, "repetition," and "working-through" are relevant to our understanding of narratives of violence. The revenant—a ghost who returns to the scene of the crime—often figures as the stand-in for a violence that cannot be overcome, or possibly even named. The ghost has a way of speaking that which cannot be spoken; it personifies and expresses those peoples, events, or aspects of one's own past that have been violently disappeared or repressed. History itself returns as revenant, as Anne White-head points out in her excellent study, *Trauma Fiction*. Whitehead begins with the awareness that there is something immediately paradoxical about the formulation: How can writers place into representational narratives ex-periences that are so extreme that they "resist language and representation" (3)? In this sense, a certain dose of imaginative or fictional reclaiming and renaming is necessary to give voice to the voiceless, as we will see in the dis-cussion of Toni Morrison, and both historians and novelists of trauma have deployed an array of literary techniques—gothic foremost among them—to generate complex aesthetic, emotional, and political responses to histories and events that might otherwise have gone unrecorded.

Further, as both Laurie Vickroy and Ron Eyerman assert in different ways, narrative has a meaning-making and identity-generating purpose: By re-working shattering and incoherent experiences into structured sequences, storytelling transforms episodes of violence from something debilitating into something potentially generative and productive. For Vickroy, trauma fic-tions partake of the therapeutic work of testifying and remembering, but also provide critical assessments of the social factors that have produced violence and, likewise, can delineate alternatives to the extant social order. Finally, trauma narrative generates a collective memory. The retelling across genera-tions of incidents of violence tends to produce and give collective shape and purpose to peoples whose agencies have been thwarted: Trauma narrative produces collective subjects. In his study of slavery as "cultural trauma," Eyerman isolates the shaping and productive capacities of tales handed down over generations: "Cultural trauma articulates a membership group as it identifies an event or an experience, a primal scene, that solidifies individual/collective identity. This event, now identified with the formation of the group, must be recollected by later generations who have had no experience of the 'original' event, yet continue to be identified by it and to identify themselves through it" (15). Trauma narrative, then, can be transformative: It produces memory and meaning, secures agency, situates experience, and thus shapes and mobilizes efforts to act upon, change, and potentially better a relentlessly violent world.

Many of the works I address in what follows share fully in such constitutive endeavors to rethink and renew, to generate possibility from the ashes of trauma. Yet, in *Haints,* I would also like to posit a series of fairly provocative claims about gothic discourse and contemporary American ghost-writing that draw upon but are in important ways distinct from the claims of trauma theory. I will typically deploy the language of haunting, the ghostly, and the gothic in what follows for a number of reasons. First, trauma theory, regardless of whether it situates trauma as "a structural disorder" or "a historical event" (Ramadanovic 199) is a theory of violence as exceptional; it partakes, thereby, of a sort of structural optimism. That is, the narratives that recount traumas figure it as a violent interruption of the seeming or normal placidity of everyday life and hold forth the hope (if never the full promise) of an imagined or imaginative recovery—a return to normality, however changed, strengthened, or tempered. Within gothic idiom, however, the provisional recovery or return to health of a traumatized individual or social body remains an open question: Gothic sets forth the possibility that there may be no way out of the labyrinthine disorientations of terror. Additionally, gothic, at its most truculent, posits the possibility that recovery or a return to health may not be desirable in the first place, insofar as "health" is quite possibly a misnomer, an alibi, which shields us from recognizing the ubiquitous banality of evil or the omnipresence of horror. As Colin Davis reminds us in his study of haunts in psychoanalysis and deconstruction, however much popular fictions strive to assure us that our ghosts are safely buried, their ubiquitous presence discomfits our singular assurance that we have survived, that we are alive. From a gothic point of view, ghosts are constitutive of everyday (rather than exceptional) subjectivity. "The subject is haunted even before it is bereaved," asserts Davis; "its engagement with others already exposes it to the reality of loss" (158). In gothic books, paintings, films, and songs, furthermore, the normal and functioning social body is often figured as already diseased and terror taken more or less as an existential given. For gothic, then, catastrophe is not at all unusual—it is familiar. That is, the horrors of trauma are not exceptions or interruptions of the quotidian social realities but rather constitute their very ground. As in a Stephen King novel, terror is not a product of the exotic or unfamiliar. Rather, it emerges in the most comfortable and familiar of everyday places—shopping malls, automobiles, suburban homes. Trauma theory, then, as it is most often deployed, depends on a possibly untenable distinction between the "normal" and the shockingly violent or disruptive.

As a corollary to this "exceptionalist" or "deviational" understanding of violence, there is a necessary tendency in trauma theory to reduce ghosts or other seemingly supernatural manifestations to the *merely* psychological, to treat hauntings as products of the traumatic events or their subsequent repression, even if they are occasioned by real historical violence, however disremembered or discounted. Yet, and although I am dealing primarily with literary fictions in what follows, I want to remain generous and open to the *real presence* of ghosts. The ghosts in the books I will discuss paradoxically demand that they be hailed and recognized as genuine presences, even if they are not fully material. Ghosts exist not simply in the imaginations of characters, but in their own right; they are possessed, so to speak, of a potent character and autonomy of their own. Ghosts have legitimate power, articulate real pains and desires, and refuse fully to be explained away as figments of diseased or troubled imaginations. Further, just as ghosts trouble the boundary between life and death, they mark inter- and extracultural boundaries. These ghosts emerge at and often *as* the very disjunctures between a hypermodern and rationalist Western social order, on the one hand, and the displaced but thriving remnants of peasant or urban folk cultures, which "modernization" so often aims to stifle, dismiss, and subdue. In the gothic works I will consider, ghosts in every way refuse to be reduced to figures of or for the pathological. They're here.

Third, trauma theory tends to understand structures of violation and recovery as universal. That is, there is a consistent underlying pattern of violence and therapeutic recovery that is understood to be common to each experience of pain and violation. Judith Lewis Herman acknowledges this explicitly in her classic feminist clinical study, *Trauma and Recovery*: "because the traumatic syndromes have basic features in common, the recovery process also follows a common pathway. The fundamental stages of recovery are establishing safety, reconstructing the trauma story, and restoring the connection between survivors and their community" (3). At the risk of sounding cold-blooded by quibbling with the great necessity of such work today among the ravages of war and exile, this seems at best undertheorized to me, if not in a way somewhat unjust. For, if we can and must acknowledge that every experience of suffering is unique, and if we accept the premise of radical cultural differentiation—that the specific content of experience is contingent upon distinct and varying social circumstances—there is no compelling reason to assume that the underlying patterns of trauma and recovery are structurally similar from case to case. The emotional trajectory of someone who has survived the Holocaust, for example, may be entirely different from that of someone who has survived the killing fields of Cambodia, or genocide in Rwanda, or been assaulted on the streets of an American city. Patterns of trauma and recovery may differ radically from war to war, violation to violation, individual to individual. Partly because it is in engaged in the good work of understanding and assisting those who have undergone extremes of violence and suffering, trauma theory tends of necessity to overgeneralize and universalize the radical uniqueness of pain and suffering. If hauntings, however, are descriptions of the return of a repressed trauma, they nevertheless insist upon their own specificity and uniqueness; which is only to say that most of the ghosts in the gothic works I review herein resist exorcism.

Finally—and this is a fairly tricky point—trauma theory, for all of its attentiveness to the ways in which violence shatters our workaday sense of causality and the flow of time, is itself swept into a historicist and causal conception of human experience that gothic singularly refuses. The return of the repressed in trauma theory may take on the form of a ghost, but it is viewed as manifestation of either a real or imagined experience that is too painful to remember or recount. Yet the ghosts in gothic works are much more than the metaphorical imagery designed to bring to consciousness the shaping force of repressed or forgotten or unnamed historical crimes. American haunts are also figures of another potential history and another potential America; they conjure up not only a forgotten history, but a more ghostly history that has never been allowed to happen. Throttled in the cradle, the ghost of a murdered infant manifests itself as the shade of an adult. Haints are also ghosts of potential: We are haunted not just by horrifying events that *have* happened in our lives or communal histories, but by histories that have never been accorded the opportunity to take place. Ghosts are revenants of a violent past, certainly, and are also spectral wavering images of potential alternative pasts.

Additionally, we are haunted by potential futures. If contemporary American gothic writing is haunted by a past that is either repressed, rewritten, abandoned, snuffed out, or mythicized, I will argue, it also speaks of and to a contemporary moment, as Jacques Derrida implies, that is "unhinged" by the future, which is why this study will focus on writing at and around the turn of the millennia. In addition to all of the characteristics the preceding critics have pointed to, in addition to the ghosting of historical determinism that gothic writing effects, *gothic*, as I will provisionally define it, is a genre singular in its ethical and epistemological open-endedness. Surely, traditional gothic writing haunted the Enlightenment pursuit of knowledge and order. So, today, it re-emerges with the eclipse of the American century, in the seeming collapse of the pretense that America be an unequivocal "force for good" across the globe.[3] Gothic is, perhaps, the most apocalyptic of fictional genres, and so is truly fitting of the "national mood" at the millennium's hinge and into the twenty-first century. For gothic, as I will demonstrate in chapter 3, promises no resolution, no assurance that the universe inhabited or the world described come with any moral guarantees that the forces of order, good, or clarity will ever triumph; gothic shatters the fantasy of justice that underwrites so much cultural production and traditionally nourishes the moral bases of social stability, from the Old Testament to national constitutions to Hollywood films. In gothic works, we can never be assured that virtue will be rewarded, vice punished, or justice delivered. More radically, we might say, as virtue and vice confuse themselves in the funhouse of mirrors that is the gothic homestead, even the bargain-basement promise of understanding is also evacuated. That is, gothic subverts the very rationale of minimal self-awareness, long the privileged Nietzschean gambit of twentieth-century realism and modernism: If there is, in fact, no sense or order to be made of the world, the realist acknowledges, at the very least, we might come to *know* that God is dead, come to *know* who we are in our collective isolation, who we are in our sadness and incapacity, and so cultivate ways to live actively and generously, if mournfully, in the awareness of our own solitude. But contemporary gothic delivers nothing of the kind, offers not even this minimal epistemological solace; it frustrates our very will to knowledge and to self-knowledge, just as it frustrates our faith in nation.

And, as the critic Mark Edmundson notes in his 1997 survey of an ubiquitous everyday gothic, *Nightmare on Main Street*, the fin de siècle culture of 1990s America (and, I might add, beyond) seems almost entirely a culture of gothic: "Gothic conventions have slipped over into ostensibly nonfictional realms. Gothic is alive not just in Stephen King's novels and Quentin Tarantino's films, but in media renderings of the O. J. Simpson case, in our political discourse, in our modes of therapy, on TV news, on talk shows like *Oprah*, in our discussions of AIDS and of the environment. American culture at large has become suffused with Gothic assumptions, with Gothic characters and plots" (xii). "Horror," Edmundson perceives, "has hit prime time—and it has stayed there. During the last decade of the century (and millennium), horror plays a central role in American culture. A time of anxiety, dread about the future, the *fin de siècle* teems with work of Gothic terror and also with their defensive antidotes, works that summon up, then cavalierly deny, Gothic fears" (3). Unsurprisingly, then, and even more acutely, as this is a cultural condition that has no doubt been exacerbated in the wake of the terror attacks of September 11, 2001, Edmundson's inquiry will call for an investigation of such symptomatic spectacles as the *X-Files* and all the Simpsons—O. J. and Homer and Jessica—as well as such highly publicized weird phenomena as "recovered memory," satanic cults, fetish clubs, and child abuse, alongside critical interrogations of the celebrated works of writers as varied as Anne Rice, Toni Morrison, and Tony Kushner. Contemporary gothic, I argue, is, as Edmundson intimates, a cultural formation specific to the perceived acceleration of catastrophe within American life. It speaks to and of our unhinging, our precarious condition today.

In my own focus on ghosts and the ghostly in US literature from the 1980s to the present, such endemic works will spur a meditation on *lack* itself—the not there—in contemporary America. My keyword, *haints,* thus combines a distinct regional pronunciation of the word *haunts,* or ghosts, with the traditional corruption *ain't.* Ghosts are haunt and ain't; ghosts are the nonexistent, the ain't, the other: They ain't both in the sense that they are immaterial or fugitive presences of the exiled and the abandoned, and they ain't in Fei's sense that they have seldom secured an honored place in the American cultural imagination. How do cultural representations of ghosts permit or even produce powerful meditations on those aspects of our existence that find no recognition elsewhere? How do ghosts allow us to speak the unspeakable? If Fei's observation is apt, we might ask, *why* have we no reverence for an accumulated past? To what extent is this future-oriented outlook a uniquely American phenomenon, and to what extent is it a consequence of what historians and sociologists term processes of "modernization" or "Westernization"? What anxieties do we encounter today, as that typically bumptious American orientation toward the future becomes troubled? What, if anything, has changed about "American eyes" since 1944?

For, as Eric Savoy in turn has pointed out, there is something resolutely and "distinctively *American*" at work here,

> in the strange tropes, figures, and rhetorical techniques, so strikingly central in American Gothic narratives, that express a profound anxiety about historical crimes and perverse human desires that cast their shadow over what many would like to be the sunny American republic. Espe-

cially important in this tradition of verbal devices is *prosopopoeia,* or personification, by which abstract ideas (such as the burden of historical causes) are given a "body" in the spectral figure of the ghost. It is also the strategy that enables the dead to rise, the ghostly voice to materialize out of nowhere, and objects to assume a menacing pseudo-lie. It thus achieves the ultimate effects of the haunted, the uncanny, and the return of the repressed while placing these thoroughly in the depths of the American life and the American psyche. ("The Rise of American Gothic" 168)

In this book, I examine some of the tenuous footholds ghosts *have* gained in the United States over the course of the last half century or so. For a literary critic, indeed, contemporary American gothic writing presents an embarrassment of riches. For the sake of presenting a more or less streamlined argument, consequently, in what follows, I have scanted more writings than I have addressed in detail; some of the works I have slighted are mentioned briefly in my conclusion. As I consider this work to consist of a series of what I hope are provocative commentaries on our cultural condition, additionally, I have kept footnotes to a minimum. In my defense, I can only point to the ongoing critical work in the field, some of which I cite, much of which is still emerging. I hope as well that my own contribution to the discussion proves as productive and contentious as those to whom I am indebted. The first chapter lays out the contours of what I envision as a generalized theory of a deeply haunted American identity. Chapter 2 considers writings of the past few decades that have used images of ghosts and the gothic form more generally to consider the painful burdens of American pasts that refuse to stay dead and buried. The third chapter of *Haints* discusses apocalyptic gothic, a literature, I argue, that marks the conclusion of an American century and the withering away of an American national project, catapults us into a new and paradoxically productive and terrorizing unknown. I want to listen acutely to what ghosts *can* say, to consider critically the genuine cultural work that ghosts do in American life today. My project is taken up partly at the instigation of the sociologist Avery F. Gordon, who in her pathbreaking 1997 study, *Ghostly Matters,* asserts that "haunting rather than history (or historicism) best captures the constellation of connections that charges any 'time of the now' with the debts of the past and the expense of the present" (142).

What are the debts of the past? And what is the expense of the present? What is it to be haunted, to live as haunted (tragically, perhaps, or comically), without ever fully recognizing that we are in the thrall of ghosts? How does gothic imagine futurity? And how can such a rarefied scholarly enterprise as

literary and cultural criticism help us to measure—or even begin to repay—
the largely unacknowledged burden of our immense historical debt? Given
the severe pressures of the contemporary world, the burdens of daily life and
given, too, how each of us struggles to survive the rapid and ongoing trans-
formations of political, military, economic, and social institutions in our own
backyards and across the globe, how is a modest investigation of culture even
relevant today?

1
Haints and Nation
Ghosts and the Narrative of National Identity

Culture and Hauntings

Let me begin, then, with a brief propaedeutic discussion of the role and purpose of "culture" in contemporary life. Critics of "multiculturalism" and the
emerging discipline of "cultural studies" lament that *culture* is a term so vague
and ephemeral as to be emptied of all precise meaning. Critiquing the tendency in cultural studies to short shrift economic analysis, for example, Russell
Jacoby carps about "the refusal or inability to address what makes up a culture" (38) on the part of American intellectuals. Jacoby's query raises a multitude of questions. To whom does a culture belong, and how does cultural
experience change over the course of generations? What is a business culture, for example, and how can one distinguish the cultural elements of business as it is lived and practiced from the purely economic? Do distinct patterns of cultural behavior characterize the practices of insiders merely, or all
those affected? Does a business culture include consumers? Is a warden part
of a prison subculture? Are the guards? What about the spouses and family
members of the inmates? If I use Microsoft Word to write this book, am I an
active participant in the kind of corporate culture espoused and largely defined by a single figure, Bill Gates? Or am I positioned outside or even against
that culture if I use his word processor to type up an indictment of his business practices for a court briefing? If I use the Internet to research the brief,
am I thereby on the fringes of the culture of geek technocracy? What, we
might ask, is a religious culture, or an ethnic, linguistic, geographic, class, or
political culture? Where are its limits? Do Spaniards participate in the same
"Western" culture as Koreans who have moved to Vancouver? Are radical Is-
lamicists who drive SUVs, play golf, accumulate wealth, and patronize strip
clubs truly, irreducibly, at loggerheads with Protestant individualism? Does

multiculturalism denote a collection of various overlapping groups of people sharing the same political and geographic terrain? Or, does it describe the complexity and contradictory range of the various "subject positions" a single individual adopts over the course of a day or a lifetime? Can one not be, say, an aging, devout Jewish entrepreneur, who is politically engaged with liberal causes? Does she not share the same "American" culture as, for example, a twenty-something, conservative, Roman Catholic, African American industrial worker? Or an atheist, Spanish-speaking, socialist migrant? If culture is merely a question of how beliefs and values are coded and represented, lived, practiced, and passed on over the course of generations, what distinguishes the "cultural" from the "social"? Or, when we speak of cultures, are we talking simply about our deepest and most cherished values, those values that we may only recognize in situations of crisis? Finally, and most pertinent to my investigation, we face the problem of a "national" culture. Does it even make sense today—did it ever?—to speak of an "American" culture or cultures? *Culture* turns out to be a term equally as unstable as the terms *gothic* or *America.*

Jacoby, a utopian progressive, for his part insists that we in America (and in the West) share a common culture, that our similarities more than outweigh our differences. When this argument is made from the right (as recently by Samuel Huntington), we should be suspicious: In such a work as *Who Are We: The Challenges to America's National Identity,* Huntington is simply trying to exclude those peoples of different skin color, religion, or social history from participating in the shared social contract of modernity and democracy. As Goddu has warned, a consolidated national culture is a culture of exclusion, which is to say, in Derridean terms, haunted. Yet there is no reason that the groups who negotiate social contracts be culturally homogenous—indeed, there is every reason to believe exactly the opposite (because in a culturally homogenous society, there would be no need for any social institutions to protect the contract). Moreover, such insistences echo earlier arguments that civilizations belonged to and were transmitted by certain privileged classes or, in the nineteenth and early twentieth centuries, races: Peasants, Jews, Irish, gypsies, blacks, Indian "savages," and other disparaged groups were understood to be excluded (and self-selectively excluded) from the benefits of modernity. The hugely violent upheavals and wars of the twentieth century, wars that, sadly, have continued unabated into the next, might best be understood as massive efforts to "homogenize" populations—typically under the political alliance of the empire or the nation-state—by exiling or exterminating undesirable elements, ensuring that the nation and its territories be composed of people who are "just like us," who "share our values," or at least can be bribed or compelled to. "Shared values" is quite probably the most dominant cliché of contemporary neo-imperialism, an imperialism that, however warm and fuzzy its rhetorical slogans, seldom shows anything like its human face. If modern gothic, as I contend, marks a new kind of haunting, then we will number among its ghosts those who have been slaughtered or displaced by the violent work of modernization, cleared from the land and cleared from—or rewritten mythically into—consciousness. With respect to the American enterprise, for example, Renée L Bergland, concurring with Goddu's contention that American self-representations have striven to repress material and social realities, documents in detail how American writers, following an imaginative corollary to Andrew Jackson's Indian removal policy, have insistently and repeatedly "ghosted" Indians: "By writing about Indians as ghosts, white writers effectively remove them from American lands and place them, instead, within the American imagination" (4).

But the slaughter, real and representational, shows no sign of abating. Understandably, then, the investigation of "who belongs?" culturally to any given social organization or institution is far from an abstract theoretical query; rather, the answers provided to such questions—Are you an insider or an outsider? Are you one of us, or an alien? Are you with us, or against us?—have profound, even life and death, consequences. Nor are they simply political; they are deeply rooted in our everyday bodily practices. I'd wager that the struggle to formulate and provide answers to such questions takes up most of our limited supply of everyday energy. All day, and every day, we articulate and negotiate our own complex identities by improvising upon a cultural repertoire that, in turn, draws on a range of preexistent options. Obviously, the arena of culture is not exhausted by the traditional art forms of music, dance, literature, or the visual arts. The clothes we choose to wear; the television shows, movies, concerts, or sporting events we choose to watch; the forms we fill out when applying for a home or car loan or a new credit card or a new country; the individuals we are comfortable gossiping with or seducing; the language and accents we speak—all are cultural practices that define us. Through such cultural practices we aim to know and to *advertise* who we are, to secure and locate our place within a larger community. The "culture wars" pop critics used to speak of in the eighties and nineties are not simply questions of what to teach in a given curriculum; culture is co-extensive with every aspect of our life, from how we make love to whom we kill and imprison to whose lands and burial grounds we occupy. Wars may be fought over resources—that is, for economic reasons. But all wars are also culture wars: The ways in which living human beings are compelled to fight them always depend on the cultural mobilization of perceived and radical differences between an "us" and "the enemy." A military war over "values" is a culture war, quite literally.

Moreover, humans fight wars, real wars, precisely when the status of "who we are" is uncomfortably in question, which is why every modern war has been mobilized on at least two fronts: There is the enemy outside against whose troops our weapons are trained, and there is "the enemy within," who must be rooted out and exposed for the traitor he or she actually is, usually by covert operations and various human and technological mechanisms of surveillance. The infringements of liberty infamously codified in the Patriot Act, for example, are not simply a product of the excesses of an autocratic Republican administration, as civil libertarians would argue, nor does the Obama administration represent a simple return to civility or normalcy. Rather, such prescriptive descriptions of an enemy within are integral to the militarization of society; the conjuring up of internal aliens is absolutely essential if a country is to fight a war, because, as a collective, we are moved to violence when we are traumatized, when our identity is open to doubt.

In other words, cultural practices seem of immense urgency when our collective or individual *identities are understood to be threatened*—that is, when we are compelled to recognize how shaky are the cultural props we have forged and secured in order to bolster our sense of privileged and unshakable identity. Immediately after the attacks of September 11, 2001, for example, there was, understandably, a good deal of public stress on America's "unity." The attacks killed a great number of people and solicited many questions. Such events stir us to ask: Who are we? and What are we doing? To prop up a national identity perceived to be under threat, the media (along with other institutions designated responsible for maintaining collective public discourse) championed national unity rather than emphasizing the many and profound differences and disagreements among our people. Across America, people participated in interdenominational prayer services, queued up to give blood, and flew the flag, symbolically demonstrating that we were a nation united.

And yet, ironically enough, in the few short years since the attacks, "our" differences appear to be even more sharply defined than ever, and seem, despite ongoing efforts on behalf of bipartisan solutions, more and more insurmountable. There seemed little, if any, common ground or sense of shared values, for example, between those Americans who were stirred by the attacks to question—deeply, widely, and intimately—America's global role in the post–Cold-war era, and those in whom the national humiliation and trauma of September 11 spurred little more than blind patriotic fury and bloodlust, culminating in a thirst for any revenge, however misdirected. That is, in the aftermath of September 11, the various ways in which the question of American identity was framed (and potentially answered) dominated the ideological landscape of the United States (and, in a profound sense, the entire world) during the first decade of the twenty-first century. "Who are we?" became, once again, the most urgent of questions, although the left and the right deploy a very different rhetoric in asking it. Evidently, it is a question some of us, at least, have been willing to kill and to die for, in wars that have now lasted nearly a decade.

Let me recount a personal episode that may help illustrate my point. In 2003, in an "Introduction to Literature" course offered at Oklahoma State University, I devoted a September 11 anniversary class to artistic responses to the attacks. To my dismay, I found in my research that, at the time, only a handful of poets and almost no fiction writers have penned compelling or forceful responses to the event. The literature of 9/11, it appeared, had yet to be written, though this situation is now beginning to change, with the appearance, mostly by male writers, of such works as William Gibson's *Pattern Recognition* (2003), Jonathan Safran Foer's *Extremely Loud and Incredibly Close* (2006), and Don DeLillo's *Falling Man* (2007). My early sense of the artistic neglect of September 11 might be accounted for by the inadequacy of my research; or it may have been simply a function of time and gestation: Such traumatic events as the September 11 attacks may take years for us to digest and more years until powerful artistic meditations can be generated. Ultimately, one aim of this book is to contend that contemporary gothic literature does speak cogently, if indirectly, to the sensibilities and conditions of which the attacks and the American response were symptomatic.

More troubling, however, is the possibility that the sort of literature I am paid to teach will have very little to say to us. It may well be that poets and novelists no longer perform the same social function as they have in centuries past. That is, the poet may no longer address her voice to a "national" or even a collective audience; novelists may today solicit our response as ethical individuals, rather than as members of a larger—let alone a national—community. If so, this points to an immense sea change in the very premise and project of cultural production. Over the second half of the twentieth century, as I have argued elsewhere,[1] cultural production has taken on a wholly novel social role, abandoning its modern mission of participating in the fabrication of national subjects. Novels, the key technology in the national social apparatus of the nineteenth and early twentieth centuries, have become increasingly marginalized over the past fifty years (which is not to say they are not read, but simply that they are read differently). In the postmodern cultural arena, it may instead be popular and commercial artists who address us most poignantly in the collective, who speak to us not as distinct individuals but as member of a specific target community: a particular age group, for example, or ethnicity or race, or country (and I believe this is true even in the digital age, as cultural consumption becomes more and more a process of individuated cultural production). "Serious" poets and writers address individuals; because their performances are driven by sales, however, popular entertainers speak directly to *audiences*. In fact, even though several observers have pointed to the postmodern collapse of distinctions between the "highbrow" and the "popular," in a consumer age where flexible niche-marketing has replaced standardized mass production, the size of one's audience and the extent to which any cultural performance acknowledges to whom it is speaking may provide the best working definition of the popular. It is no accident that new *films* are emerging, which do powerfully engage the events of September 11: Michael Moore's *Fahrenheit 9/11* (2004) is the most celebrated example; *United 93* (2006), *World Trade Center* (2006), and *Reign Over Me* (2007) are others, despite their various fortunes at the box office. As a cultural formation, cinema positions itself precisely in the borderlands between the popular and the artistic.

To speak of a "postnational" era, then, is certainly not to posit the disappearance of nations, nor of national identities; rather, it is, modestly enough, to suggest that the claims upon our identities made today by *nation* are one set of affiliative claims among many. At any rate, to return to my anecdote, the paucity of literary responses to the attacks threw my students and me into the domain of popular music. For all their banality, many popular singers, I would claim, still feel it their place to speak to us—plaintively, angrily, consolingly, excitedly—*as Americans*. So together, as a class, my students and I looked at songs we had heard that best captured our complex emotional responses to September 11. But this realization too led us to an impasse: I wanted to listen to Bruce Springsteen's *The Rising*, while my students from Oklahoma wanted to listen to their favorite native son, Toby Keith. For Keith, a "boot up the ass" is the "American way," as he put it in his notorious "Courtesy of the Red, White and Blue (The Angry American)," which reached number one on the country charts. Springsteen and Keith offer two very different takes on the attacks and speak to a deep split in American sensibility, as Stanley Kurtz of the highbrow conservative *National Review* opined in an online column: "Bruce or Toby? Is rueful lament a better answer to 9/11 than robust anger?" An important cultural question, I would think. Now, I am of a different generation than my students ("Bruce who?"), and we are from different regions of the country ("Toby who?"). I was raised on Springsteen's

Rust Belt, immigrant, working-class laments, and they are very close to my heart. Springsteen speaks of and (perhaps) to a class and a generation that was and is deeply invested in the "American dream"; but Springsteen's target audience has recognized that this dream has either failed them or that they have failed it. The American dream may come true, his songs say, and I hope it does, because it is a beautiful dream. But it sure does not seem to be coming true for us! My students, however, do not often listen to Bruce Springsteen. Why should they? And how can an old fart like me respond to a pop musician like Toby Keith? Despite country and western's traditional project of recording the exuberant disillusionment of poor rural whites displaced to the city (listen to the cowboy "swing" of Bob Wills and the Texas Playboys sometime, or the honky-tonk of Hank Williams), contemporary popular country and western seems stubbornly to resist acknowledging class defeat. Patriotism has always trumped disillusionment in white working-class music. Even so, sometime in the late 1970s or early '80s, country and western's time-honored sentimentalism got happy and naïve and lost all its sense of irony (Ronald Reagan and Merle Haggard are no doubt the key transitional figures in this evolution, although Reagan—irony of ironies!—claimed to be a Springsteen fan). To be fair, another immensely popular country singer, Alan Jackson, offered a much more sober impression of September 11, even though his popular song "Where Were You (When the World Stopped Turning)" availed itself of a rather timid and conventional sentimentalism, so too did the Dixie Chicks' open criticism of President Bush suggest there is anything but unanimity in Nashville. Such ideological frameworks are anything but stable and, as cultural theorists point out, they deploy "empty" signifiers that are constantly subject to renegotiation. Keith himself, of late, endorsed Barack Obama's bid for the presidency. Of course, everyone has different tastes in popular music, and those tastes are historically and socially situated. But popular songs—what we like, what we listen to, what we hum in the shower—are undoubtedly among the most powerful ways in which we articulate *who we are*. Whole subcultures define themselves almost entirely—for example, politically, ethnically, generationally—by their taste in music (and this is true, I think, for many of us, not simply the young).

Moreover, I find both Keith and Springsteen relevant to my discussion of ghosts, for both artists are engaged in the task of publicly honoring and addressing the dead; both speaking to the trauma of "nation." Gothic, as William Veeder has stressed, is both subversive *and* popular. Central to my argument throughout *Haints* is the claim that no individual or collective identity can be forged without reference to the dead—both those dead whose sacrifice and loss we honor and recognize and whom we mourn and bury honorably in the walls of our cities, and, *more critically,* those dead we forget, dismiss, or despise: the enemy dead or the unburied, the hordes of the nameless dead, whose disappearance clears the ground for our living existence, those dead *haints* who nonetheless lay claim to our being. All sentimentalism aside, trauma, nation, the dead, and the public role of culture will be key terms of my own critical investigation. An identity "in question," I will argue, is a "ghosted identity"—and the cultural and political questions raised have to do with who we are in relation to our dead. How can we accommodate haunts? How can we *live* in the proximity of ghosts? Put one way, the question I will be asking throughout this book is, how do we bury our dead? Put another way, the question I will be asking throughout is how, outside the relatively artificial space of the classroom, can we responsibly and responsively *listen* to each others' music?

You might respond that anyone's taste in popular music is not only a superficial matter, but culturally epiphenomenal. You might like Britney Spears and I might like Dr. Dre, and someone else might like bagpipes. But we are all sitting together in the same classroom, or in the same church, or, at the very least, in the same state or country or continent. Moreover, as Jacoby would argue, all of these musical styles implicitly celebrate the same values despite their seemingly different emphases. Whatever the explicit subject of a song's lyrics, at heart, all popular music pays tribute to the same set of values: lust, a seemingly universal love of rhythm, celebrity-fetishism, the cultural domination of a technocratic elite in the guise of consumerist democracy, corporate sponsorship of the "counterculture," and so forth. All popular culture today is, if not innately capitalist, swept into the orbit of capital: Artistry is subservient to profit. Even so, culture still matters. Across the globe, popular music is taken, for better or worse, as a powerful signifier for "Western"; and MTV and its spin-offs, as handmaidens to American economic hegemony, are in the business of nothing so much as marketing "Western lifestyles" internationally. More pointedly, country music, wherever it is performed or listened to, and given how taste is structured and marked by class, has replaced jazz as the iconographic *American* music, and it is appreciated or despised insofar as the American "values" it seems to embody and endorse are championed or rejected. So, to echo Kurtz, the compelling question is: who is more *American,* Bruce or Toby? Here at home, the disagreements that emerge from such a "dissensus" in popular culture are of genuine consequence. Fans of Toby Keith will hear an elaborate justification of retaliatory war against the nearest convenient enemy; fans of Springsteen, I hope, remembering his political track record, will be considerably more cautious. Each group is laying claim to a highly contested sense of national identity.

And, as Kurtz and other conservative commentators rather gleefully point out, the divide between bellicosity and caution may in fact be the sharpest division in post-9/11 America. For all their faux-populist chatter, however, conservatives (including their contemporary "tea-party" offspring) are profoundly mistaken (or perhaps profoundly disingenuous) to see this divide as a split between a namby-pamby liberal elite and a vigorous populist muscular patriotism. On the contrary, in retrospect, it seems that it was virtually the *entire* ruling elite acting as one—Democrats and Republicans, politicians, bureaucrats, corporate oligarchs, and the mainstream media—who conspired to commit the country to a misguided war in Iraq, against the wishes and better judgment of a powerful and surprisingly large grassroots antiwar movement. The antiwar coalition was likewise peopled by those with a remarkably wide range of ideological affiliations, which may only suggest that ideology, though far from dead, is the messiest of things. Obviously, there was a groundswell of heartland patriotism after September 11. But the precise consequences of such sentiments are always an open political question: The cultural performance of placing an American flag bumper sticker on your car to bolster and advertise who you are does not amount to an explicit or even implicit endorsement of the invasion of Iraq, or at least it did not until the Bush administration convinced us that Saddam Hussein was behind the attacks. Such patriotism might just as well have been used to endorse a war against less convenient enemies: Pakistan, say, or Iran, or Saudi Arabia, had the Bush people cared to point out that most of the hijackers were Saudi nationals. What *matters*, then, is the ways in which such sentiments are politically channeled (and, as I argued earlier, culture is a prized mechanism for the political channeling of sentiment). Of course, elite warmongers affiliated themselves tactically with "the people" just as the antiwar movement enlisted the assistance of a few progressive elites (and whatever their ostensible popularity, we must remember, national wars are always dictated and controlled from the top, as only a very small handful of people have the authority to order troops to mobilize). Unfortunately, like my students and me, the two groups seemed to have no common language whatsoever.

Where was our shared culture then? Both sides were willing to talk, it seemed, but neither was willing to listen, and so, ironically, the president's imperial claim that you were either with us or against us became perfectly justified. In such a context, charges that dissenters are guilty of "anti-Americanism" are absolutely consistent, even key: What cultural conservatives are laying claim to is the cultural concept of America itself, which has little, if any, necessary connection to policy. Those of us in the antiwar camp, to whom it seemed patently obvious that the hawks and neoconservatives, along with all their misled fellow travelers, were hell-bent on dismantling damn-near *everything* good in the American tradition, could only shake our heads and mutter Tonto's response in the punch line to the old joke about the Lone Ranger and Tonto surrounded by hostile Indians: "What do you mean 'we,' white man?"

I think it is a mighty good question: What *do* we mean by "we"?

Culture—I am hardly alone in pointing out—is precisely that performative dimension of our lives that addresses this urgent question. That is, culture maps the terrain on which identity is investigated, negotiated, rejected, transformed, articulated, killed over, and, on occasion, transmitted. Surely culture is entangled with such economic realities as, for example, class; but, for the purposes of my argument, we can make the rather banal point that a class *culture* would be those aspects of behavior and performance that signify or grapple with the specific problem of class *identity*. Culture reads and writes and shouts and dances and sings—performs, in short—and *listens to*—an "I," an "us."

The very term *culture,* as Raymond Williams has stressed, has a particularly vexed political genealogy. I would like to address the question "what *is* culture?" by reformulating it from a pragmatist perspective: What does culture *do?* The pragmatist philosopher, when faced with a phenomenon for which she feels compelled to account, will not consider the essence or being of that phenomenon. Rather, she will try to understand its *function*, asking not "what is it?" but "what does it do?," "what new things does it make possible?," or "what realities does it construct?" This problem will form the starting point of my investigation: *What does culture do today?* Culture does many things, but most of all, it *does* identity. Culture, like Shakespeare's greatly haunted *Hamlet*, begins with the question, "who's there?" "Who am I?" it asks. "Who are you?" "Stand and unfold yourself" (*Hamlet* I.i.2). Cultural phenomena (e.g., movies, songs, books, performances, architectures, lifestyles, foods, clothes, habits) never simply dictate to us who we are, although many cultural manifestations and artifacts betray an autocratic impulse to tell us our place, to assign us a distinct, definite, and highly rigid and limited role in the world. More powerfully, cultural performances, as Judith Butler has argued with respect to gender and sexuality, provide the stage whereon—and a set of props by which—identities might be perpetually negotiated and improvised. Culture, we might say, is an immense machine engaged in the production of heterogeneous and constantly fluctuating identities. And identity is more process than product. Like Hamlet himself, identity is always and everywhere improvised, theatricalized, negotiable, fluid, vexed, and, more often than not, contradictory. It is never replete nor complete, never accomplished, never wholly known to itself. Identity, as deconstructive philosophy argues, is predicated on and constituted by that which it excludes; a self is never an autonomous entity, but is distinguished by the line of demarcation that separates itself from what it *is not*. This is what Derrida suggests when he speaks of "radical alterity": at the root is the other. To use his later terminology, *identity is haunted*. The most compelling and powerful cultural performances today, I would argue, are those that share in the community of the dead, rather than those that exile our ghosts. Culture matters precisely because it offers ways of living with and among identities in question, with and among our *haints*. Edmundson, then, to return to some of my earlier observations, is asking the most demanding and pointed of questions: "What cultural work is contemporary Gothic doing for its consumers? Why do we need it?" (xiii). And how does gothic "do" America?

The Cultural Imperative: Jamaica Kincaid's "Girl"

As a rather lovely illustration of the complex ways in which culture *does* identity, let me turn to Jamaica Kincaid's much-anthologized short story, "Girl," originally published in the *New Yorker* in 1978, which inaugurates her first collection, *At the Bottom of the River*. Though Kincaid is not always considered a gothic writer (her work is often characterized as surreal), her protagonists are deeply haunted by their pasts in the islands, and this haunting typically becomes the occasion through which they strive for self-sufficiency and autonomy. *Annie John,* her first novel, which tells of the eponymous narrator's growth to maturity and independence and chronicles her various loves and friendships en route, opens with the child's visions of the dead: "I was afraid of the dead, as was everyone I knew. We were afraid of the dead because we never could tell when they might show up again ... [S]ometimes they would show up standing under a tree just as you were passing by. They might follow you home, and even though they might not be able to come into your house, they might wait for you and follow you wherever you went; in that case they would never give up until you joined them" (4). "My mother died at the moment I was born, and so for my whole life there was nothing standing between myself and eternity" (3) reads the opening line of *The Autobiography of My Mother,* and Kincaid's memoir recounting her brother's death of AIDS concludes: "I wrote about the dead for the dead" (197). *At the Bottom of the River* is chock full of *duppies*. The second story, "In the Night," gives us "the woman who has removed her skin and is on her way to drink the blood of her secret enemies" (6), the sound of another woman's "spirit back from the dead, looking at the man who used to groan" (7), and "Mr. Gishard, standing under a cedar tree which is in full bloom, wearing that nice suit, which is as fresh as the day he was buried in it" (7); the collection closes with "death on death on death" (68) of the final titular vignette.

The presumably nongothic text of "Girl" is composed largely of a string of commands and injunctions designed to assign the eponymous protagonist a very precise gender location within a dominant cultural regime: "Wash the white clothes on Monday and put them on the stone heap; wash the color clothes on Tuesday and put them on the clothesline to dry; don't walk bare-head in the hot sun; cook pumpkin fritters in very hot sweet oil" (3). The addressee/protagonist of the story, "Girl," who seems to be on the cusp of adolescence, is given a precise set of instructions, consisting largely of practical and folk wisdoms pertaining to women's assigned domestic duties. Do this; do not do that. She is taught how to cook and to clean and to care for her man "this is how to iron your father's khaki shirt so that it doesn't have a crease" (4). We know that this story takes place in a colonial or postcolonial society (the khaki uniforms), in Antigua or somewhere in the Caribbean (she is told not to sing "benna," a kind of calypso song, and she learns how to grow okra and "dasheen," to prepare "doukona" and pepper pot, to catch fish). Women's work, the culture dictates, is household work; to be a woman is to know and practice these things. In this series of utterances and commands, the character Girl emerges as the spoken (to). She does not preexist the cultural commands that dictate who she is, just as, by Jacques Lacan's argument, we do not preexist the language into which we are born. *The language, the culture, speaks us into being.* Girl cannot exist as a person prior to the commands that summon her into being. She is given a set of instructions that tell her who she is, domestically, physically, and sexually: "Don't squat down to play marbles—you are not a boy, you know" (4–5). She is instructed in sexual wiles—"This is how to smile at someone you don't like at all" (4)—and folk remedies: "This is how to make a good medicine for a cold" (5). The voice speaking, a kind of matriarchal cultural superego, is transmitting a complex set of time-honored practical skills to her daughter or perhaps to her grand-daughter. Girl's identity is formed by learning what it is to be a woman, to know her place. She is being told (by her mother) who she is.

It is key to remember, however, that the culture that speaks us into being is neither univocal nor unidirectional. In other words, our culture "speaks us into being" with many quarrelsome voices, and we are everywhere speaking back to it, giving it lip. "Language," write Gilles Deleuze and Félix Guattari, "is made not to be believed but to be obeyed, and to compel obedience" (*A Thousand Plateaus* 76). "The elementary unit of language," Deleuze and Guattari argue, is what they call the "order-word" (76), whereby any statement does not so much convey information as assign the listener a precise place and identity with a pregiven linguistic and, we would say, cultural order. But such order-words cannot be taken "straight," because, as with any imperative, the medium is the message. All sorts of interferences and ambiguities accompany the transmission of the seemingly clear set of instructions. If the set of commands in Kincaid's story are dictating to Girl her identity, then they are also implicitly acknowledging that it is no simple thing to "be" or to become a girl. To begin with, Kincaid highlights the glaring contradiction between the "essential" identity being assigned and the very need for identity education. If Girl *is* a girl, why does she have to *learn how* to be a girl? If you are what you are, why do you need to learn how to be it? Femininity, in such a culture, turns out to be anything but essential, something the mother speaking in this story knows very well, presumably without ever having read Joan Riviere or Judith Butler. The feminine is an entirely theatrical construct: "This is how to hem a dress when you see the hem coming down and so to prevent yourself from looking like the slut I know you are so bent on becoming" (4). Moreover, this theatricality is patently hypocritical. It turns out that to be what you are (a lady) is in fact to be what you are not, or rather, to *not appear to be* what you are (a slut). At least twice the daughter is told *not* to be what she is, a logical impossibility: "On Sundays try to walk like a lady and not like the slut you are so bent on becoming" (3); "This is how to behave in the presence of men who don't know you very well, and this way they won't recognize immediately the slut I have warned you against becoming" (4). To *be* a lady is, precisely, *to not be what you are.* To be a "lady" is to be a hypocrite, although there is no genuine hypocrisy involved, as everyone should fully understand the game being played (though Girl, for her part, remains incredulous). The overt message is "you are a lady, act like one!" The covert, but obvious, message being communicated is "you are a slut!" (and so Girl is being carefully initiated into women's "essential," but culturally dictated, sense of sexual shame). But the message is, deliberately, it seems, mixed. There may be another, more approving injunction, winkingly given here: "Go ahead and be a slut, just don't let men see that you are one." The overriding cultural message then might be something like this: "To be a lady *is* to be a slut, and every woman knows this, so you can't fool me and you best not try to fool yourself, and after all there is nothing wrong with that, so go ahead and enjoy it, but best pretend not to, given the place we're living, and maybe you can at least fool some of the men." After being told to behave like a lady and not a slut, Girl is told quite plainly how to trigger a spontaneous abortion, and so erase the social signifier of her sluttishness, a child born out of wedlock: "This is how to make a good medicine to throw away a child before it even becomes a child" (4). In this sense, Girl is being introduced to a very specific kind of women's empowerment, a kind of black-magic or home remedy for enduring and surviving the patriarchy, a certain set of women's secret skills that should never be revealed to anyone but one's own daughter. To be a woman is to be shamed and empowered at once.

The set of ambiguous and contradictory instructions through which Girl is assigned her social, class, and sexual place is deeply embedded in the culture, terrain, and history of the island. This set of instructions in "girl-hood" is written like an accent into her very body, in a more-or-less Foucauldian way, as she is instructed how to walk, how to talk, how to smile. Our deepest natures, like the languages we speak and the accents and intonations in which we speak them, are complex cultural and bodily performances of a socially inscribed identity.

There is an identifiable Caribbean accent, which varies from island to island, town to town, family to family, and yet everyone's individual voice is unmistakably unique. I sound a lot like—but not identical to—my brother. And, like the distinct and singular intonations of our unique voices, every cultural performance we engage in is a radical improvisation on the script we are assigned. We perform our cultures through back talk. Our culture preexists us, and we are scripted into it; yet, as Foucault points out, there is no power without resistance. Every individual cultural performance is unique. In some sense, even, the rebelliousness and contentiousness is already prewritten into the script. Consider Kincaid's matriarchal superego. Does she expect Girl to acquiesce to the cultural expectations of womanhood? And if so, to which ones, insofar as femininity is a complex performance of *seeming to be* without being? Is the speaker slyly encouraging her daughter's sluttishness or shaming her daughter? Given her constant badgering, can the mother figure here realistically expect her commands to be obeyed? Or does the mother know full well that her nagging will incite a rebellion? Will the daughter's inevitable (I think) rebellion be sullen, resentful, self-loathing, and reactive? Will Girl's adult identity always be smothered by her mother's insistent, persistent voice? (One student of mine has suggested that the entire story "Girl" is a dramatic monologue, taking place in the head of a woman who has interiorized her mother, a mother that has never, will never, allow her fully to mature.) Or will the daughter's rebellion be total, active, joyous—will she grow up a daring feminist and reject all the hidebound sexist rules of her native culture and write her own life story, her own cultural identity, according to rules that she herself invents? And, paradoxically enough, could this be what the mother secretly wants her to do? If the mother is teaching that womanliness *is* deviousness, will she be displeased or encouraged by her daughter's rather devious response? What, precisely, is Girl's potential? *What is* she to be?

For it turns out that, if this text, like *The Autobiography of My Mother,* like all of Kincaid's writing, I would venture, is "mother-haunted," it is also deeply haunted by the ambiguous prospectus of one's own destiny and potential: identity is both scripted in the flesh, and radically open to countless revisions; every improvised performance of who one *is* constitutes a unique material variation on who one was *told to be;* the essential is no more than eventual, and thereby open. Girl, for example, responds in her "own" voice twice in the story, interjections marked in italics by Kincaid. Her responses are significant. The first deploys a child's logic: "*But I don't sing benna on Sundays at all, and never in Sunday school*" (4). Here Girl is both refuting and conceding the identity being assigned her. "I don't do that," she answers her mother when accused of singing benna on Sundays, "that is not me." The mother's charge is thereby unjust. Girl continues, however, with a covert but rather explicit admission of guilt. Why would she insist that she does not sing in Sunday school, unless she is implicitly admitting that her mother's charge is, in fact, half true? She does, she seems to confess, sing benna at other times of the Holy Day.

At the very conclusion of the story, Girl protests again, and this time the mother responds: "Always squeeze bread to make sure it's fresh; *but what if the baker won't let me feel the bread?;* you mean to say that after all you are going to be the kind of woman who the baker won't let near the bread?" (5). Girl's response is hypothetical and conditional ("what if?"), signaling that she is expanding on her mother's commands and assuming, on her own initiative, responsibility in the outside world. Commands, she has learned, and rules of behavior, will only take her so far. As someone who has to make do for herself, she must adapt those lessons in real-life situations and confront the imperatives of situational ethics. Further, her mother's rules all insist that she conform to authority (do this, her mother enjoins; do not do that). How, the girl wonders, should she meet the strictures of outside (presumably male) authority, when purchasing fresh bread is both a domestic and a public or economic activity, an activity, no less, in which her identity is being judged as singularly related to public perceptions of her sexual behavior? Such is the lot of all women, her mother is warning her. But then, asks Girl, out in the world, is she supposed to resist being assigned her "place," or should she assert her rights within that place? Mother responds, as bad mothers sometimes do, by taking the opportunity to demean her child yet again. After all I've told you about how to behave, you still insist on being a slut, do you? (The mother figure, of course, disregards what she has previously stipulated, that the Girl will be a slut, no matter what she is told; why then, would she be surprised?) Yet there are positive signs here too; in this exchange, Girl asserts her own independence to the extent that the mother is forced to recognize it and respond to it. Further, her mother's rhetoric has changed in an important but subtle way. Not only does she respond to Girl, but her response implicitly assumes Girl's right to be what she—Girl—decides for herself. Even while diminishing her daughter's self-esteem, the mother implicitly acknowledges the child's right to independence. And, she leaves the question open: What kind of woman are you going to be? Who are you? The question is left open, undecidable, and if we read the story optimistically, we see that there is plenty of elbow room here for Girl to articulate her own response to the question, as she grows and lives.

The gendered performance being demanded by the mother and the cultural dictates about womanhood that the mother espouses are, at the very least, double-voiced: to be a woman is to be two contrary things at once and to cultivate the contradiction; the cultivation of such contradictions, a lesson quickly learned and seized upon by Girl, enables her to fully renegotiate—and quite possibly reject—the terms of the social contract, with the assistance of no other agent but herself. The self, however, is not fully present to itself: It is ghosted both by the voice that speaks it, her mother, in this case, and ghosted, too, by its own radically open future.

Souls in Pain Know No Borders: Isabel Allende's Invented Country

A ghost, consequently, is a figure of cultural displacement and dislocation, who haunts the very disjunction between one's assigned location within a given social regime and one's willed refusal, forced removal or exile, and exploration of alternative modes of existence. In *A Small Place,* in *Lucy,* in much of Kincaid's work, the protagonist's eventual move to America involves a way of negotiating one's ghosts, appeasing them, settling them. In America, as Fei insisted, the ideal is to live in the present and the future, to refuse cultural dictates, to give up one's ghosts. Indeed, as I will argue, the various models of assimilation and "Americanization" worked through (and often rejected) by immigrant and ethnic literature situate themselves precisely within the ghostly. As Kathleen Brogan argues, with respect to Cristina Garcia's haunted novel of generational displacement, *Dreaming in Cuban,* in narratives of exile and immigration, "a real place becomes merely a ghostly memory, whatever importance it has bestowed only by those who have left" (127). To become American is to seize your own destiny and assume responsibility for your identity and our future; to become American, *ideally,* is to give up your ghosts, by becoming future-oriented instead of past-oriented, and so to have the debts of the past written off. For Brogan, however, assimilation will culmi-

nate not in renouncing the past, but rather in reintegrating it through a successful process of mourning: "The proper conclusion of mourning involves
the 'translation' or the incorporation of the past into the present, a positive
'haunting'" (127).

The deeply haunted Chilean exile and expatriate writer, Isabel Allende,
states the case succinctly in her memoir of national loss and political dislocation, *My Invented Country*.[2] In Chile, she asserts, one dwells with and among
the past, lives daily among ghosts:

> I didn't inherit my grandmother's psychic powers, but she opened my
> mind to the mysteries of the world. I accept that anything is possible.
> She maintained that there are multiple dimensions to reality, and that
> it isn't prudent to trust solely in reason and in our limited senses in
> trying to understand life; other tools of perception exist, such as in-
> stinct, imagination, dreams, emotion, and intuition. She introduced me
> to magical realism long before the so-called boom in Latin American
> literature made it fashionable. Her views have helped me in my work
> because I confront each book with the same criterion she used to con-
> duct her sessions: calling on the spirits with delicacy, so they will tell
> me their lives. Literary characters, like my grandmother's apparitions,
> are fragile beings, easily frightened; they must be treated with care so
> they will feel comfortable in my pages.
>
> Apparitions, tables that move on their own, miraculous saints and
> devils with green hooves riding on public transportation make life and
> death more interesting. Souls in pain know no borders. I have a friend
> in Chile who wakes up at night to find tall skinny visitors from Africa
> dressed in tunics and armed with spears, specters only he can see. His
> wife, who sleeps right beside him, has never seen the Africans, only two
> eighteenth-century English gentlewomen who walk through doors. And
> another friend of mine lived in a house in Santiago where lamps mys-
> teriously crashed to the floor and chairs overturned; the source of the
> mayhem was discovered to be the ghost of a Danish geographer who
> was dug up in the patio along with his maps and his notebook. How
> did that poor wandering soul end up so far from home? We will never
> know, but after several novenas and a few masses for him, the geogra-
> pher left. He must have been a Calvinist or a Lutheran during his life-
> time and didn't like the papist rites. (69–70)

Her new American home, however, has no space allotted for such nonsense. Yet, "in the United States, in contrast, the past doesn't matter; no-one

asks your last name; the son of a murderer can be president . . . as long as he's white. You can make mistakes because new opportunities abound, you just move to a new state and change your name and start a new life. Spaces are so vast that the roads never meet" (191). Nevertheless, even in the most patriotic of immigrant literature, one seldom gets off the hook so easily (and Allende, who holds the United States largely responsible for the vicious coup that deposed and killed her uncle, President Salvador Allende, on September 11, ironically enough, 1973, is hardly a tub-thumping patriot). Rather, in her writing, as in so many of the cultural works I examine in *Haints,* the process of "becoming American" appears to present an entirely new dilemma of hauntedness. To begin with, in America, one is situated in a deeply heterogeneous society that, as Fei argues, has no designated cultural place for ghosts. That is, "our" traditions and rituals and common practices provide little space for us to pay reverence to our dead: consider, for a moment, the haste and solipsism with which funerals are generally performed in this country. In her epic of assimilation, exile, and return, *China Men,* Maxine Hong Kingston offers a telling anecdote of the mythical procedures of integration: "In another family, a grandfather came to one of them in a dream and said that the kids were to bury their parents correctly; after that they would be absolved of all duties to ancestors since they were now Americans" (189). Consequently, our ghosts—and they are legion—are compelled by force of necessity to improvise new modes of address: They must continually reinvent the space from which they speak to us, as does, in fact, the grandfather in the family Kingston describes.

Allende and her American husband, for example, go through an elaborate "renovation" of their California home in order to entice ghosts there with the simulacrum of antiquity: "My husband and I have built a large house in northern California with high ceilings, beams, and arches to invite ghosts from various periods and latitudes, especially those of the far south. In an attempt to replicate my great-grandparents house [Allende's model for her first book, *The House of Spirits*], we have aged it through the costly and laborious process of attacking the doors with hammers, staining the walls with paint, rusting the iron with acid, and treading the plants in the garden. The result is rather convincing: I believe that more than one distraught spirit might settle in with us, deceived by the look of the property" (70).

The neighbors gape, of course, and Allende insists that her house is "a historical impossibility" (70). And yet, there the house is. What after all, could be more "American" than fabricating an "aged" house based on one that once existed in Chile? What could be more Californian, more downright Hollywood? In America, it turns out, "anything is possible," much more so, per-

haps, than in Chile: History itself is open to renegotiation. By the end of the
memoir, in fact, readers—and Allende herself—come to recognize that the
United States, no less than Chile, no less than literature itself, is "the invented
country in which I live" (198). It is not a question of Americans having no history, exactly, or tradition; rather, it is a question of our *history and tradition
being radically improvisational;* because of the deeply multiethnic makeup
of our nation, further, and because of the revolutionary violence necessary
to isolate our disparate cultural ghosts in the name of our common national
future, American ghosts will be highly ingenious, mobile, and ethnically in-
flected, as we shall see. If, in fact, "souls in pain know no borders," America,
in some sense, serves metonymically to absorb the global eclipse of tradition.
The displaced dead throng here as exiles, just like the living: "In the United
States, everyone, with the exception of the Indians, descends from someone
who came from somewhere else," observes Allende; "The twentieth century
was the century of immigrants and refugees; the world has never seen so
many humans fleeing violence or poverty abandon their place of origin to
start a new life in a new land. My family and I are part of that diaspora" (187).
Allende's self-portrait in this book is, after all, a character who is doubly exiled: She is a political refugee from Pinochet's Chile, haunted by a country
and a past that, for most of the narrative, she can only revisit in her imagination. So too, and consequently, she is a sort of internal exile of America, as
many first-generation immigrants are condemned to live in a country whose
proudest values are those of national and individual self-invention. In some
sense, all Americans—immigrants and natives, whose access to their own
various pasts has been forcibly denied for most of the country's history—are
haunted. We are haunted not because we honor our pasts, but precisely *because* it is so difficult to do so in a place where our eyes are turned straight
ahead. Our dead are haints, much more so than in Europe, Africa, Asia, or
Latin America: They ain't here, and in their ain't-ness, are legion. In the move
to America, they mark both a discontinuation and a refabrication of an absent or fading cultural heritage. The house, the American home, certificate
of the American dream accomplished, must, as Savoy intimates, be haunted.

The house she builds with her husband, after all, is the invention or simu-
lation of a forged past, and such a Hollywood feat of the imagination is only
thinkable, in some ways, in polyglot America, where one's past is so radically subject to renegotiation. If you come to America fleeing your past, it is
simple enough to invent a new past in order to secure for yourself a profitable future, like Jay Gatsby did. The second part of my study's subtitle, "millennial passions," refers to another pole of the supernatural in American culture and suggests that the ghostly in America haunts and beckons us from

the apocalyptic potential of our futures, imagined and unimaginable. The haints figured in fictions of the sixties, seventies, eighties, nineties, and into the new century, I argue, have an implicit if seldom fully articulated relation to the turn of the millennium, for that date serves as a powerful signifier of the radically and dangerously open nature of the future. But in all of the works I examine, the identities performed are ghosted by a future that they are in the process of inventing. The American ghostly, I contend, signifies a relative liberation from historical servitude: It is a ghost of alternative, of potential, of possibility. This potential may damn or destroy us, as in the apocalyptic gothic I will turn to shortly; it may, alternatively, lead to salvation of a sort. In either case, it haunts us relentlessly; it demands an *encounter*.

Ghastly Selves and the Ghost of a Dollar: Henry James's "The Jolly Corner"

I draw my next illustration from a very different register, but it too is a different kind of immigration story, a story of exile and repatriation that confronts us with a ghostly and a ghastly America. This example too involves a dramatized meditation on the ghostliness of destiny and potential, which similarly meditates on longing, national exile, and return. In Henry James's classic 1908 ghost story, "The Jolly Corner," a man is haunted by his own alter ego, an alternate, potential, and quite powerful version of himself. James's familiar theme here is the fate of old money in the turn to the business economy of the gilded age; he writes in the heyday of American realism, at the turn of the last century, when realism, as envisioned and championed by William Dean Howells, involved an ethical commitment to American democracy. Yet if Howells's project emphasized verisimilitude, it appears paradoxical that many of our classic realists—James, Edith Wharton, and Ambrose Bierce leap to mind—were also splendid writers of ghost stories. It can be claimed that these realist ghosts in their stories are psychological manifestations of repressed aspects of the self and represent a return of repressed desires. Fair enough—the great insight of the psychological realists was to recognize, as in Wharton's homoerotic story "The Eyes," for example, that the self *is* a ghost.

At fifty-six, James's protagonist, Spencer Brydon, has just returned to his home in New York after twenty-three years away, to look after his properties, most importantly, "his house on the jolly corner, as he usually, and quite fondly, described it" (314). He finds New York, and by extension, the United States, to have become, in his absence, "vulgar and sordid" (315), grotesque, shallow, and materialist. Meditating on how his life might have been different had he stayed in the States and become an entrepreneur and real estate developer, he declaims to his love interest, Alice Staverton, that "there are no reasons here but *of* dollars. Let us therefore have none whatever—not the ghost of one" (319). Of ghosts, he admits, when she remarks on his turn of expression, "the place must swarm with them" (319). Indeed, his house on the jolly corner will turn out to be haunted.

In some sense, as with all of James's writing, the story is describing competing understandings of "value," and therefore competing struggles for cultural identity. Twentieth-century American capitalism represents the triumph of restless commercialism, and those who give themselves over to its pursuits turn out, inevitably and inescapably, to be acquisitive, superficial, boorish, and gauche. In an ironic homage to Frederick Jackson Turner, James uses an explicitly Darwinian language to describe the rather brutalized making of Americans. For those whose values are measured in terms of the refinement of their sensibilities—their taste, conversation, wit, and cultivated intimacy with the profounder depth of human experience—such crass commercialism must be rejected. Like Brydon, the Jamesian hero typically finds a kind of refuge in Europe. Yet to read James merely as a champion of old world refinement over new world philistinism, I think, is profoundly to underestimate his work. Quite often, his novels and plays end up endorsing an Emersonian American vitalism in the face of a potentially menacing European and aristocratic decadence, as with *The Portrait of a Lady,* perhaps, or, arguably, *The American.* At his best, James is not endorsing one way of living—European sophistication—over the other—American philistinism—so much as he is investigating what is fully at stake in the lived encounter between the "American" and the "European." "The Jolly Corner" describes the mutual haunting of these two selves; the ghost Brydon encounters will be a vision of his own self had he stayed in America.

Though all of James's writing struggles with the problem of passion and sexuality—Brydon will have to tangle with the apparition before he can consummate his long-deferred love for Alice Staverton—at least three other important considerations are mutely at work in his tales and novels: the consequences and corruptions of wealth; the fallible and self-deceiving nature of subjective consciousness; and the question of American political destiny. All of these concerns are intricately bound up with one another, I believe, and all are immediately at stake in his remarkable ghost stories. To put it summarily, we could say that the central question James dramatizes in all of his writing is whether the self is fully knowable; his most powerful works depict the shattering encounter of the self with its own unknown, which is to say, a haunting. Importantly, however, I want to insist that his ghosts are not merely psychological manifestations, as most commentators seem to understand them. They are "real" ghosts, genuine presences, although ghosts are not simply the disembodied dead. Much more than that, in James, ghosts are the palpable presence of that which is absent, that which is unknown, that which has been exiled from the subjective mind and the community in order that a "working" apprehension of the real might be secured. The much celebrated, deeply ironized, Jamesian "point of view" is purchased (if you will permit me to pursue the economic metaphor) after a long bargaining with ghosts. That is, a properly Jamesian sensibility indulgently and sensuously celebrates that which it can perceive and describe *only* in the full, if tragic, knowledge that our sensual accommodation of the real world is limited. James's characters are haunted because what they know and hold dear to their hearts is ghosted by the unknowable, by the sacrifices they have made to cultivate the little, spare, space of perception they have carved out of the limitless chaos of experience.

The "ghost of a dollar," then, serves as an apt phrase. Dollars secure one's identity and pay for the "good life," the life of cultivated sensibility that James endorses. But the precise source of funding for one's life and adventures is always unmentionable: You can be proud of at least a moderate wealth, in James's fictional world, but the source of wealth is always an embarrassment (which is why capitalism, according to Marx, amounts to nothing less than an irrational and ghostly mysticism). James is not, by any stretch of the imagination, a proponent of the labor theory of value, of course; there are no "rational" theories that might explain the production of wealth and thereby exorcise, as Marx aims to, the ghosts of dollars by analyzing how capitalism shrouds the origins of wealth in mystification. The precise source of wealth is the central and most cherished mystery in every piece of writing by James, most notoriously in *The Ambassadors,* where the manufactured item, the source of the aptly named Newsome's wealth, literally cannot be mentioned. Rather, wealth is ghostly, and James is more interested in the unpredictable effects of money on individual subjectivity than he is in outlining a social theory for economic justice. His fictionalized Europeans, in actual fact, are often just as driven by the pursuit of wealth as are his Americans and suffer from the same shallowness of soul because of this—witness the malevolent Madame Merle in *Portrait of a Lady.* Many of them are certainly more mercenary than his Americans, and thereby, often less noble of character. The European sensibility, generally, is both literally and figuratively impoverished in his books. By the late nineteenth century, the feudal aristocratic system of obtaining wealth from land has almost entirely disappeared, and so his European characters are always out to marry and defraud the American nouveau riche. James's American characters, for their part, have seldom become rich by their own labor; workers will find themselves too much enslaved by the pressures of everyday living to cultivate the refined sensibilities he so loves. James is economically savvy enough to see that even the "self-made" man is one who gets rich off the works of others; he is a manager and a capitalist, rather than a worker. The ideal, however ironized and compromised, would seem to be to live more or less modestly, on a modest income, as has Spencer Brydon.

Brydon has lived well enough off the rent from his inherited properties to go to Europe and live life on his own terms. A representative of old money, a social order whose decline is famously documented in Wharton's *The Age of Innocence,* he has been comfortable rather than rich and has never had to worry about money. This has allowed him to live graciously. He has not had to work for profit, and he has rejected the business life embraced by others in his class and age group: "He was the owner of another, not quite so 'good'— the jolly corner having been, from far back, superlatively extended and consecrated; and the value of the pair represented his main capital, with an income consisting, in these later years, of their respective rents which (thanks precisely to their original excellent type) had never been depressingly low. He could live in 'Europe,' as he had been in the habit of living, on the product of these flourishing New York leases" (314). Brydon has been able to have his cake and eat it too; he can live well off his real estate income, without giving his life over to investment and speculation, or thereby surrendering his soul to the pursuit of profit: "If he had but stayed home he would have discovered his genius in time to really start some new variety of awful architectural hare and run it till it burrowed in a gold-mine" (316). Because of this, he can disavow the source of his wealth, and distinguish, rather artificially, between his "home"—the house on the jolly corner to which he is sentimentally attached—and his "property." When Alice Staverton accuses him of indulging in sentimentality because he could afford to—his "ill-gotten gains" allow him to be sentimental—he explains that, "even if another dollar never came to him from the other house he would nevertheless cherish this one" (318). And yet, Staverton's charge is exactly on target. By splitting his "home," or ideal sense of himself, from the source of wealth that allows him his freedom to be who he is, Brydon is propping up an insecure identity. For Brydon, the ghastly creature of the Donald Trump–like boorish billionaire is the "not me," even though the "me" is financed in more or less the same way. To exist— to sleep at night—Brydon must deny the "not me" at the heart of the "me." As with many of James's characters, his existence is a failed existence; he is haunted by the American "not me" at the core of the self, the ghastly "not me" that he has unsuccessfully attempted to purge in his years abroad. It is this self that he must confront, for it will turn out that he cannot sleep at night.

In James's work, then, identity itself is always in debt. *Identity is debt,* which is to say, it is haunted. One is "possessed," we might say, by one's possessions. Subjectivity is expense; the self is haunted by what it jointly owns and disowns, by what it cannot know or speak of itself, of others, and of the other in the self. Let me conclude this discussion, briefly, by examining a few key aspects of the encounter between the self and the ghost self in "The Jolly Corner." The encounter, it seems, cannot be evaded, despite Brydon's perpetual self-questioning and nervous anxiety; it will be his inescapable destiny to confront his alter ego, who apprehends him, ultimately, at the very threshold of his own home, when Brydon is hurrying to rush out the front door in order to evade the ghost. The question posed by the ghost, "sharp . . . as a knife in the side" (334), James interposes, is whether Brydon's actual life has been worth living. By confronting his alternative self, he has to estimate his own choices, in a typically Jamesian predicament. Has Brydon's been a life richly lived, or a life evaded?

Initially, Brydon finds himself vindicated, because he sees that the ghost, whose arms are raised to protect its own visage, is unable to confront him: "For he could but gape at his other self in this other anguish, gape as a proof that *he,* standing there for the achieved, the enjoyed, the triumphant life, couldn't be faced in his triumph" (335). The critic Krishna Baldev Vaid, for example, cites this demonstration as proof that Brydon's actual life has indeed been vindicated. Vaid contests Robert Rogers's earlier claim that "'The Jolly Corner' is . . . a tragic lament for a life unlived, for deeds undone" (qtd. in Vaid 487). "To me," counters Vaid, "'The Jolly Corner' is a joyous embodiment of a life lived, of deeds done" (487). Yet the subsequent sequence in James's text would seem to lend credence to Rogers's claim that the ghostly Brydon has lived more powerfully and intensely than has the actual Brydon:

> The hands, as he looked, began to move, to open; then, as if deciding in a flash, dropped from the face and left it uncovered and presented. Horror, with the sight, had leapt into Brydon's throat, gasping there in a sound he couldn't utter; for the bared identity was too hideous as *his,* and his glare was the passion of protest. The face, that face, Spencer Brydon's?—he searched it still, but looking away from it in dismay and denial, falling straight from his height of sublimity. . . . It came upon him nearer now, quite one of those expanding fantastic images projected by the magic lantern of childhood; for the stranger, whoever he

might be, evil, odious, blatant, vulgar, had advanced as for aggression, and he knew himself give ground. Then harder pressed still, sick with the force of his shock, and falling back as under the hot breath and the roused passion of a life larger than his own, a rage of personality before which his own collapsed, he felt the whole vision turn to darkness and his very feet give way. (335–36)

"A life larger than his own"—the line seems to clinch the case. For all its vulgarity and evil, for all its nonexistence, the ghost, paradoxically enough, had lived more deeply and suffered more intensely than had Brydon.

And yet, this is not James's final word on the case. After all, Brydon seemingly survives the ordeal, and, eventually, gets the girl. Just as in "The Beast in the Jungle," the traumas of the passionless protagonist do not go fully unrecognized. That is, rather than asking his critics and readers to judge and either condemn or endorse his characters' passions, James may be compelling them to indulge the encounter. The questions—Have I made the right choices? Have I lived life to the fullest?—are as unanswerable *and* as unavoidable for Brydon as they are for anyone entering late middle age. We all ask it of ourselves; but there is no satisfactory answer, beyond an acceptance of the life choices one has made, for better or worse. To answer by saying, "I've lived beautifully" would be to display the same arrogance of Brydon, who considers himself morally superior to Americans and is limited by nothing so much as his insecurity and smugness; to answer by saying "I've lived shamefully" would be—would it not?—to perpetuate the callow dishonesty, evasiveness, and self-denial that has so far marked Brydon's fortunes. There are no right answers.

Even so, there is no escaping the question. James, to be sure, prizes intensity—of experience, of feeling, of intellect—over every alternative moral virtue. The quality to affect and to be affected, as Deleuze claims, is the only and inevitable way to live ethically. Yet, one can—and must—intensely *feel* one's failing. If Brydon is redeemed at all (and James uses exactly the theological language of redemption), it is precisely *because* of his encounter with the ghost. That is, one is compelled to live with the ain't of one's own life, to embrace, in a Nietzschean sense, what might be called the experiential gambit, which proceeds by the way of a sacrificial logic. Every time you choose the right turn, your journey down the road is "ghosted," in a sense, by the left turn you might have taken.[3] According to James's ethics, in order to experience that right turn fully, you must—at the risk of your own destruction— recognize, honor, and forget the ghost of the left, the ghost of both alternative and potential. That is, the fullness of the road on the right can only be lived in its absolute singularity, without regret. At the same time, the right road is not full unless the alternative is fully part of that experience. We exist in the space of those who are not there: the haints. How then, are we to live ghosted? If American life, for James, has any genuine failings, they do not stem simply from our acquisitiveness and superficiality; rather, they emerge from our having failed to find ways to live with ghosts.

Theories of Contemporary American Gothic

A central contention in this book, then, is that identity is, like Hamlet, deeply *haunted*. It is deeply haunted by what is past, and it is deeply haunted, as Derrida says, by a future, by what (it) might be. A theory of haunting, then, cannot simply invoke history, for hauntings summon up not merely absent pasts, but pasts that have never materialized. Our condition is deeply, doubly haunted, by what it might have been, by alternate pasts and potential presents, by the radical openness of the future and future beings. Identity is haunted by its gods, living and dead, its neighbors and friends, its enemies, living and dead. It is deeply, doubly haunted by what it is not, by the other or the "not-there," as deconstructionists and multiculturalists argue, and it is deeply haunted by intimate aspects of itself that are completely foreign, as psychoanalysis earnestly and rightly insists. And this double-hauntedness at the heart of the *I* or the *we,* I believe, is in part what Gordon acknowledges and honors when she contends that haunting describes the complexity of our debts to the past (142). So far, my argument can be summarized quite simply: culture *does* identity. Identity is haunted, indebted, or possessed, and, in large part because of our self-proclaimed exceptionalism—the belief that we have been delivered from the historical predicament—haunted in a peculiarly American sense: haunted by the multitudinousness of its pasts (actual and virtual), the alternatives of its present, and the sheer and open potential of its many possible futures. The remainder of this book will investigate the specific ways in which this hauntedness plays and is performed today, in uniquely American, gothic, and contemporary venues.

For even as we Americans are dismissive of our ghosts, we are haunted: The more we murder the past, the more it returns to make good its claims, the more these absences and omissions themselves demand reparation. "If a haunting describes how that which appears to be not there is often a seething presence, acting on and meddling with taken-for-granted realities, the ghost is just the sign, or the empirical evidence, if you like, that tells you a haunting is taking place" (Gordon 8). Even when we trace our roots, our family trees, our communal heritage, in the most humble of fashions, we *know* that we have missed something, have missed many things, perhaps everything. Lacunae, erasures, missed opportunities, the seizures of the unconscious haunt even the most Emersonian of our memoirs: the intensities and passions of a moment that are perpetually misfiled in our memory banks. Such ephemeral affects never emerge from the safe haven of short-term memory, or, if they venture on the risky journey into long-term, disguise themselves so much as to be unrecognizable.

I am speaking here of the splayed and various nature of people and communities, who everywhere resist the zeitgeists—those colonizing spirits—that want to pin them down. So too do our many pasts bubble with potentials, potentials lost and sacrificed to a historicist model. Following Derrida, we can put the assertion more strongly: The debts to our past are not only homage we owe to our ancestors, but also the heavy, heavy burdens of alternative pasts, potential presents, and unimagined futures, alternatives that have never fully manifested themselves in the stream of earthly experience. "The American Gothic narrative," as Louis S. Gross asserts in his study of the genre, offers "an alternative history of the American experience" (3). Which is to say ghosts, who haunt us seeking solace, soliciting reparations, asking that a wrong be righted, a crime be avenged, a bad be made impossibly good. The dead (with one or two exceptions) are of course beyond law. Law, which everywhere assigns limits, determines and guards borders, sentences each, ultimately, to death, has little enough to do with justice, in the Derridean sense of the term. In the afterlife, however, there is no respect for legal borders, for just limits, and so there is a voraciousness that hungers for more than anything we living might know or name as justice. And this is a heavy burden to bear. The weight of ghosts, points out the Laguna Pueblo writer Leslie Marmon Silko, speaking of the wandering souls of Yaquis butchered by Mexican forces, is almost immeasurable: "They weigh twice or three times what they weighed in life. The body carries the weight of the soul all the life, but with the body gone, there's nothing to hold the weight anymore" (*Almanac of the Dead* 191). We close our ears to such clamoring. "The place will be haunted, I suppose," writes Louise Erdrich in her most haunted (and most politically aggressive) novel, *Tracks,* speaking of the land of which the Chippewa tribe has been dispossessed, "but no one will have ears sharp enough to hear the [ghosts'] low voices, or the vision clear to see their still shadows" (204). American children hear no stories of ghosts, and ghosts, stirred by different desires, tell different stories, in different languages, than those we are accustomed to hear. The twilight landscape of terror, an endless plain, as Adrienne Rich asserts in her poetry, is infinitely larger than the map of meaning. Rich's own writings waver between a theoretical project that would exorcise patriarchal ghosts and a haunted poetry and prose that indulgently honors the victims of their crimes.

"How do we reckon with what modern history has rendered ghostly?" (18), asks Gordon, consequently, a question I am pursuing with respect to the ghostly within American culture at the present juncture, a present, as Derrida would say, peculiarly unhinged and haunted. My theme assumes the centrality of enactments of memory as popular loci of struggle over meaning within consumer culture, and targets our peculiar—if half-credited—obsession at the millennium's turn with the painful burdens of American history. I am interested in such reckonings, how cultural practices articulate individual or collective subjective sensibilities by excavating alternative histories, or "ghost" stories, by imaginatively summoning into presence those voices and beings that have been sacrificed to the march of progress and the consolidation of American literary and cultural traditions. Among other things, I want to examine the resonance of a haunted past within the context of a "multicultural" society by considering a complex of mnemonic struggles, with specific reference to the project of contemporary literature.

Much of my argument is adumbrated in Kathleen Brogan's very fine book, *Cultural Haunting,* wherein she utilizes trauma theory to posit an entirely new genre of ethnic ghost stories, dedicated to the project of "cultural mourning," which might be defined as the imaginative work communities are compelled to do wherever they are savaged by a history that both shapes and dismisses them: "haunted tales . . . bear witness to some sense of breach with the past" (23). Thus, for Brogan, who notes the ubiquity of ghosting in contemporary ethnic literature and who reads at length the tribulations of haunting in such works as Louise Erdrich's *Tracks,* Toni Morrison's *Beloved,* and Cristina Garcia's *Dreaming in Cuban,* ghosts are endowed with agency, are paradoxically powerful figures of powerlessness. They emerge at and through social gaps (both contemporary and historical), may through their fluidity and spectrality help us to reconceive "women's more restrictively defined roles as bearers of culture" (25),[4] and spur acts of cultural invention and recovery (which are not, I will insist, necessarily successful). Though I am less interested in questions of genre, I concur with much of Brogan's reasoning and hope perhaps to expand upon the perplexities of cultural haunting as it resonates with the more traditionally American theme of self-invention. Brogan stresses the involuntary nature of haunting; ghosts "figure prominently wherever people must reconceive a fragmented, partially obliterated history, looking to a newly imagined past to redefine themselves for the future" (29). And yet, by her reading, the putative or partial exorcism of the array of ghosts who solicit ethnic memory can result in, or at least point to, the "full inte-

gration" (7) of identity (both individual and communal). The trajectory followed by such writings, she argues, moves "from bad to good forms of haunting" (6). That is, these novels perform, via relatively successful techniques of
mourning, a shift from "traumatic memory," in which identity is shattered,
chaotic, immobilized, and chained to the past, to "narrative memory." Narrative memory honors and ceremonially buries the dead in all the dignity
they demand and, so, allows us to both remember and move on. In Freudian
terms, cultural mourning involves a successful "working through" of loss and
historical disenfranchisement, rather than a mere "acting out." Thus, for example, in Morrison's novel, *Beloved,* although the haunted character of Sethe
may not fully recover, Morrison's narrative itself makes good on its promise
of a cultural reintegration of an "unspeakable" memory, a savaged and "disappeared" history: "although its haunting remains unresolved, *Beloved* holds
open the possibility that readers may join the author in forming a community of mourners who commemorate the dead. The novel works to translate
trauma's community of silence (the community of characters) into a community grounded in—in fact, created by—open shared remembering (the community of its ideal readers)" (Brogan 91).

Historical Invisibilities

As Gordon argues in *Ghostly Matters,* history traces a consequential set of
paradigms that results (in a more or less determinate fashion) in the postu-
lated inevitability—or even the guilt-ridden *necessity*—of the contemporary.
Historicism, which has provided a rationale for what Gordon and others consider the deeply violent project of modernity itself, is riddled with ideology
and invokes a secular notion of causality; historicism defends the implaca-
bility of "things as they are" based on a streamlined model in which the inde-
terminate chaos of human events is channeled into a consequential, compre-
hensible pattern (the history of "peoples," of nations, of communities). The
endeavor to trace out history, we might say, is haunted, even as we are, for it
involves an effort to settle accounts with a past—a multiplicity of pasts—that
has been forgotten or erased (and, as Fei comments, Americans are stereo-
typically indifferent to the determining forces of their own past and present).
As a science, history is a complex apologia; it aims to master the polyvalent
past, to wrestle it into submission, in order to justify the naturally seeming inevitability of things as they patently are. Furthermore, according to the logic
of "historicism," as Homi Bhabha has argued, "narrative is only the agency of
the event, or the medium of a naturalist continuity of Community or Tradition" (151). Yet pasts—which must be thought of in the plural and in their im-

manent potentiality—seldom submit to our mastery, which is why historiography never tells us anything genuine about the past, but simply, falteringly, describes and tries to account for our present, as even professional historians are beginning to acknowledge.

And yet a multitude of counternarratives refute and subvert the implacable and dry logic of historical teleology. Contemporary American fictions in particular, I contend, map out a terrain for the sort of haunting that Gordon has described: a sometimes wrenching and catastrophic encounter with that beckoning Other, the dispossessed, the forgotten, the unburied, the un- or still- or half-born—that which eludes historical accountability. This—*haints*— describes and delineates an Other to which neither history nor the conventional techniques of memory, collective or individual, can fully hearken, for it refuses to assign our living and sensual being with a determinate location. Rather, hauntings beckon us elsewhere, invite us to cross over the abyss, beyond the smug certainty of life as we know it, to confront that which we can only acknowledge in the abject terror of our dread: the fulsomeness and catastrophe of the incalculable blood debts we owe to the past. Acknowledging the role of fabulation in articulating that which is absent from history and on the fringes of memory, Gordon describes the "fictive," then, as "not simply literature but . . . the ensemble of cultural imaginings, affective experiences, animated objects, marginal voices, narrative destinies, and eccentric traces of power's presence" (25). Consequently, as I have indicated, a muted but central concern of this study will be the place and social function of what is perhaps too glibly termed *postmodern* culture.

2
Memory, Race, Ethnicity, and Violence

The Labor of Memory: Toni Morrison's *Beloved*

The debts we owe the past can only be paid off through hard work, and in this chapter, I aim to demonstrate how contemporary practices of memory involve labor. Toni Morrison, whose work I will treat as a very special example, speaks of the work of memory, in an essay entitled "Memory, Creation and Writing": "Memory (the deliberate act of remembering) is a form of willed creation. It is not an effort to find out the way it really was—that is research. The point is to dwell on the way it appeared and why it appeared in that particular way" (385). Thus, "the language, if it is to permit criticism of both rebellion and tradition, must be both indicator and mask, and the tension between the two kinds of language is its release and power. If my work is to be functional to the group (to the village as it were) then it must bear witness and identify that which is useful from the past and that which ought to be discarded; it must make it possible to prepare for the present and live it out, and it must do that not by avoiding problems and contradictions but by examining them; it should not even attempt to solve social problems, but it should attempt to clarify them" (389). For Morrison, the clarification of social problems, then, is the work of historical memory, understood as creation, as fiction. In Morrison's novels, many of the characters—black and white—have been denied their own pasts, not only by the violence of slavery, but sometimes even by the violence attendant upon black emancipation. In *Song of Solomon*, for example, a free black from Georgia whose father is deceased is rechristened "Macon Dead" by a drunken Yankee who has trouble filling in the right boxes on his documents. He is left to live with the name, to build on it—his past is sacrificed. Now this is part and parcel of an American mythos of individual fortitude. The so-called American dream stipulates that one is not judged by the past—it does not matter who your folks are, whether they are rich or poor, nobility or working class. It is up to you to pull yourself up by your bootstraps and to make something of yourself as an individual. Thus, the emancipation of American blacks involves extending to slaves this so-called opportunity, regardless of the oppressive effects of social conditions, which the drama of American mobility must necessarily conspire to ignore. Americans, legendarily, free themselves by shunning the past. In *Song of Solomon,* then, two generations on, we encounter Milkman Dead, the spoiled son of a middle-class black slumlord; his father has clawed his own way from poverty and his American ambition makes him want to forget and abandon his dead. But, as so often in Morrison's work, the dead refuse the destiny of death: The bodies of the murdered women in *Paradise,* for example, simply disappear, and the characters show up, transfigured, in an epilogue. In *Song of Solomon,* Milkman will be challenged to rediscover his own roots. He undertakes a journey of discovery to the South, is symbolically divested of all the trappings of his own wealth and power, and through his trials rediscovers the heritage that had been destroyed—made dead—by the stroke of an abolitionist's pen.[1]

Because "the injustices done to the dead can never be redressed," (147), "the ethical imperative" of Morrison's writing, as Jeffrey Andrew Weinstock insists, "is for one to recognize the immensity and terrifying reality of loss. *Beloved* structures an encounter with lostness and introduces the necessity of mourning the lost as lost so as to open up the possibility of a different future. Finally, what Sethe and Denver learn to do, at the end of it all, is to live. And it is a ghost who teaches them how" (148). *Haints* is a term common in Toni Morrison's writing, and Morrison is of course a central figure. In all of her works, the dead—the past—refuse to remain buried. The pull of the slaughtered, the sacrificed, is insistent, selfish, dangerous, and its gravity works against the American myth of individualist mobility and self-reliance, of flight away from the strictures of the social. I got "a tree on my back and a haint in my house," says Sethe in the remarkable ghost story *Beloved,* a novel of repossession as well as of Reconstruction. Sethe's history is branded upon her body, in the form of a tree that has grown on her back, "a chokeberry tree. Trunk branches and even leaves. Tiny little chokeberry leaves" (17), the result of a violent whipping when she was a slave. Amy dresses Sethe's back with cobwebs, "like stringing a tree for Christmas" (80). As the novel develops, as shards of the past are told and retold by the various characters, that violent history begins to open for us, the tree begins to bloom and to bleed. "It's gonna hurt now," says Amy, a white girl who helps her in her escape, "anything dead coming back to life hurts" (35).

And trees forest this novel. A wilderness of motif throngs at the borders of any provisional solace that can be cleared in and from a past that is nothing less than a tribunal of brutality, just as the woods ring the clearing where Baby Suggs preaches, just as branches both shelter and encroach upon the bower that Denver claims as her own space: "Back beyond 124 was a narrow field that stopped itself at a wood. On the yonder side of these woods, a stream. In these woods, between the field and the stream, hidden by post oaks, five boxwood bushes, planted in a ring, toward each other four feet off the ground to form a round, empty room seven feet high, its walls fifty inches of murmuring leaves" (28). The "unspeakable" is that which is murmuring in the trees. Trees, symbols of life and force, are also menacing; they form barriers to understanding. When Paul D, for example, is unable to face up to Sethe's past, Morrison writes that "the forest was locking the distance between them" (165). "'So long,'" Sethe murmurs as he departs, "from the far side of the trees" (165). And Stamp Paid notes that trees, like the old tree he has named Brother on the Sweet Home plantation, have been sacred and holy: "Sixo went among trees at night. For dancing, he said, to keep his bloodlines open" (25). When Sixo resists capture, however, he is knocked out and "comes to, a hickory fire . . . in front of him and . . . tied to a tree" (227). As Paul D later makes his escape from the chain gang, as he wanders north traveling an illusory path to an illusory freedom, he follows the trees as the Cherokee instruct him, racing "from dogwood to blossoming peach. When they thinned out he headed for the cherry blossoms, then magnolia, chinaberry, pecan, walnut and prickly pear. At last he reached a field of apple trees whose flowers were just becoming tiny knots of fruit" (112), led at last to Sethe and 124, "a dark ragged figure guided by the blossoming plums" (113).

But in trees now live the unmourned, unburied dead, and it is "the meanness of the dead" (4) that makes Sethe's life impossible. The women working in the field hang their children in trees to be safe, but the image prefigures the lynchings to come. There are the trees of "bitter fruit" from which the slaves are hanged: "but hidden in lacy groves. Boys hanging from the most beautiful sycamores in the world. It shamed her—remembering the wonderful soughing trees rather than the boys. Try as she might to make it otherwise, the sycamores beat out the children every time and she could not forgive her memory for that" (6). Howard and Buglar, Sethe's runaway sons, habituate trees piecemeal: "When her dreams roamed outside 124, anywhere they wished, she saw them sometimes in beautiful trees, their little legs barely visible in the leaves" (39). "She saw only their parts in trees" (86). Trees have become fossilized, petrified, diabolical. The tree on Sethe's back—"not a tree" as Paul D insists, "nothing like any tree he knew because trees were inviting; things you could trust and be near; talk to if you wanted to" (21)—becomes the "wrought iron" spinal cord of bitter memory.

Dismemberment conveys the whole violence of the family saga. In a remarkable essay, Hortense Spillers outlines how the searing and violation of flesh performs the very instantiation of an exclusionary national ideology: "the social-political order of the New World, . . . with its human sequence written in blood, *represents* for its African and indigenous peoples a scene of *actual* mutilation, dismemberment and exile" ("Mama's Baby, Papa's Maybe" 67). Under slavery, where the flesh is commodified, the violent separation of mother and child enforces what might be called the diaspora of memory in the loss of self-mastery: "The destructive loss of the natural mother, whose biological/genetic relationship to the child remains unique and unambiguous, opens the enslaved young to social ambiguity and chaos: the ambiguity of his/her fatherhood and to a structure of other relational elements, that would declare the young's connection to a genetic and historic future. . . . Under these arrangements, the customary lexis of sexuality, including 're-production,' 'motherhood,' 'pleasure,' and 'desire' are thrown into unrelieved crisis" (76). This violence, which begins initially with the "theft of the body" (67), as Spillers insists (hence ghosts) is the unspeakable at the heart of a national history, an unspeakable of which literal infanticide, literal lynchings, are instantiations.

"Axe the trunk, the limb will die" (242). In *Beloved,* inevitably, dismemberment marks both the connections between the generations, between mother and child (milk, the bloodlines, the family tree, the tree of life) as well as the violation of family. Beloved wants to know about her family, her past: "Your woman she never fixed your hair?" (60). Sethe does not "remember" her mother, she tells her own daughters, all that she can recall is her mark: "She picked me up and carried me behind the smokehouse. Back there she opened up her dress front and lifted her breast and pointed under it. Right on her rib was a circle and a cross burnt right in the skin. She said, 'this is your ma'am. This,' and she pointed. 'I am the only one got this mark now. The rest dead. If something happens to me and you can't tell by my face, you can know me by this mark'" (61). Significantly, Sethe's mother lifts her breast as if to feed her child; the mark she bears on her ribcage is the only connection that can be established between the two: "'Mark me too,'" says Sethe, "'Mark the mark on me too'" and is slapped: "'I didn't understand it then. Not till I had a mark of my own.'" (61). Her mother too is hanged and "by the time they cut her down nobody could tell whether she had a circle and a cross or not" (61). But Sethe will get her mark: the chokeberry tree cut into her back, the mark that unites her with her mother in the violation of their very right to be joined. And, at her whipping, it is the violation of the mother and child relationship that is for her most traumatic, as she explains to Paul D:

> "Schoolteacher made one open up my back, and when it closed it made a tree. It grows there still."
> "They used cowhide on you?"
> "And they took my milk."
> "They beat you and you was pregnant?"
> "And they took my milk!" (17)

Blood and sap and milk and nourishment and urine: blossoming. Both Denver and Beloved will likewise be branded with this heritage. Sethe attempts to kill her children in the woodshed, significantly: "A pretty little slave-girl had recognized a hat, and split to the woodshed to kill her own children" (158). Afterwards, "Sethe was aiming a bloody nipple into the baby's mouth" (152). When Beloved later emerges from the stream, she leans "against a mulberry tree" (50); she is found "'sleep on a stump" (235), and has marks on her throat, which may perhaps be from the saw with which the infant was dispatched. Later, as Denver, who "swallowed her blood right along with my mother's milk" (205), leaves 124 and solicits the community's help, her growth is marked by trees: "Letters cut into beeches and oaks by giants were eye level now" (245). *Beloved* is in some sense Denver's coming-of-age story. After her venturing forth, local women leave food for the family "on the tree stump at the edge of the yard" (249).

Through a wholesale institution of almost ritualized scarification, a specific form of underground cultural memory is fabricated, in an almost Nietzschean fashion. Spillers explains:

> These undecipherable markings on the captive body render a kind of hieroglyphics of the flesh whose severe disjunctures come to be hidden to the cultural seeing by skin color. We might well ask if this phenomenon of marking and branding actually "transfers" from one generation to another, finding its various *symbolic substitutions* in an efficacy of meanings that repeat the initiating moments? As Elaine Scarry describes the mechanisms of torture, these lacerations, woundings, fissures, tears, scars, openings, ruptures, lesions, rendings, punctures of the flesh create the distance between what I would designate a cultural *vestibularity* and the *culture*, whose state apparatus, including judges, attorneys, "owners," "soul drivers," "overseers," and "men of God," ap-

parently colludes with a protocol of "search and destroy." This body whose flesh carries the female and the male to the frontier of survival bears in person the marks of a cultural text whose inside has been turned outside. ("Mama's Baby" 67)

Inside out, like a ghoul's flesh. Denied access to any sort of officially authorized voice, this vestibular culture of memory brutalized has no choice but to haunt. What Sethe calls *rememory* in this book, the insistence of the unspeakable, is both blessed and tortuous, a mixture of scarification and love. But rememory is not simply a private haunting, a trauma, for the past lingers in ways that all of us in the present can stumble across, as Sethe explains:

"Some things you forget. Other things you never do. . . . Places, places are still there. If a house burns down, it's gone, but the place—the picture of it—stays, and not just in my rememory, but out there in the world. What I remember is a picture floating around out there outside my head. I mean, even if I don't think it, even if I die, the picture of what I did, or knew, or saw is still out there. Right in the place where it happened."

"Can other people see it?" asked Denver.

"Oh, yes. Oh, yes, yes, yes. Someday you be walking down the road and you hear something or see something going on. So clear. And you think it's you thinking it up. A thought picture. But no. It's when you bump into a rememory that belongs to somebody else." (36)

Historical memory is the very agonized nexus between self and community. Consequently, according to Lois Parkinson Zamora, "ghosts carry the burden of tradition and collective memory: Ancestral apparitions often act as correctives to the insularities of individuality, as links to lost families and communities, or as reminders of communal crimes, crises, cruelties. They may suggest displacement and alienation or, alternatively, reunion and communion"(497).

The occult is—quite literally—the hidden, the covered over, which does not arise simply, as if in a historical vacuum, from the repressed desires of individuals. Rather, ghosts may be historically situated and produced as that which cannot be said—the unspeakable—in order for the fantasy of nation to maintain itself. Infanticide, a condensation of the many unspeakable "sins" at the heart of *Beloved,* is a symptom of the precise historical pathology that would permit the fugitive slave act. In "The Site of Memory," Morrison explains how a historically violent exclusion underwrites the imperative that she, "a writer in the last quarter of the twentieth century, not much more than a hundred years after Emancipation, a writer who is black and a woman" interrogate the unspeakable, the occult: "My job becomes how to rip that veil drawn over 'proceedings too terrible to relate.' The exercise is critical for any person who is black, or who belongs to any marginalized category, for historically, we were seldom invited to participate in the discourse even when we were its topic" (110–111). The site of memory—the haunted place—inhabited or occupied by the creative writer affiliated to traditionally marginalized communities stands in contrast to those sites, however fabricated, that might once have been authorized by a common tradition.

Given the difficulties of producing a fantasy of a "national" heritage in so large, heterogeneous, and complex a country as the United States, "a country of plural memories and diverse traditions" (Nora 287), and an achievement, at best, of staggering violence, we are afloat rather than rooted in history. In his own formulation of the sites of memory, Pierre Nora insists on their fragmentary and ghostly nature: "there are *lieux de memoire,* sites of memory, because there are no longer *milieux de memoire,* real environments of memory" (284). These sites are "moments of history torn away from the movement of history, then returned; no longer quite life, not yet death, like shells on the shore when the sea of living memory has receded" (289). Consequently, we are compelled to remember, as Nora elaborates, considering the "atomization of a general memory into a private one" (292). The past has become radically other: "only in a regime of discontinuity are such hallucinations of the past conceivable" (293). Under the combined pressures of democratization, decolonization, and mass cultures, "we have seen," he writes, "the end of societies that had long assured the transmission and conservation of collectively remembered values, whether through churches or schools, the family or the state; the end too of ideologies that prepared a smooth passage from the past to the future or that had indicated that the future should be kept from the past—whether for reaction, progress, or even revolution. Indeed, we have seen the tremendous dilation of our very mode of historical perception, which, with the help of the media, has substituted for a memory entwined in the intimacy of a collective heritage the ephemeral film of current events" (284–85).

Consequent upon what Jean-François Lyotard has famously termed the *breakdown of metanarratives,* then, in which local practices and customs might once have secured their rationale within a presumably universal unfolding of the destiny of a nation, tribe, or common humanity, mnemonic practices (prayer, festivals, the veneration of saints or ancestors), become increasingly distressed. We are no longer able to live securely "within memory" (285), Nora writes. For Nora, this "rupture of equilibrium" wherein "the remnants of experience still lived in the warmth of tradition, in the silence of custom, in the repetition of the ancestral, have been displaced" (284), compels communities to endlessly refabricate a complex of representational customs that self-consciously acknowledge themselves as precarious, as threatened. Paradoxically, memory, which knows itself as spontaneous, subjective, passional, must everywhere be reconstituted: "our memory, nothing more than sifted and sorted historical traces" (285).

According to Nora, history and memory have been placed in "fundamental opposition" (285). "History . . . is the reconstruction, always problematic and incomplete, of what is no longer. Memory is a perpetually actual phenomenon, a bond tying us to the eternal present; history is a representation of the past. Memory . . . is affective and magical" (285). And yet, memory has been radically uprooted:

> *Lieux de memoire* originate with the sense that there is no spontaneous memory, that we must deliberately create archives, maintain anniversaries, organize celebrations, pronounce eulogies, and notarize bills because such activities no longer occur naturally. The defense, by certain minorities, of a privileged memory that has retreated to jealously protected enclaves in this sense intensely illuminates the truth of *lieux de memoire*—that without commemorative vigilance, history would sweep them away. We buttress our identities upon such bastions, but if what they defeated were not threatened, there would be no need to build them. (289)

Memory thus opens itself to a politics, a contestation; moreover, as Nora implicitly acknowledges, the figuration of such tensions demands an irrepressibly gothic vernacular: the language of the haunted. He himself characterizes such sites as ghostly, even ghastly: "moments of history torn away from the movement of history, then returned; no longer quite life, yet not death, like shells on the shore when the sea of living memory has receded" (289).

In *Beloved,* for example, Sethe suffers at—and from—the very disjunction between lived direct memories, which are habitual, somatic, as the chokeberry tree on her back, and indirect representational memories: the stories that circulate about her. Both scar. The nexus between the two, between the personal memory one struggles with and what we might call her assigned mnemonic location within the community, is her offspring, the sacrificed daughter who returns to haunt her, greedily. So Sethe is condemned to memory. Here we are at the jammed crossroads where memory, literature, ethnicity, and the mother's loss meet to mourn.

Nora writes: "Our interest in these *lieux de memoire* that anchor, condense and express the exhausted capital of our collective memory derives from this new sensibility. History has become the deep reference of a period that has been wrenched from its depths, a realistic novel in a period in which there are no real novels. Memory has been promoted to the center of history: such is the spectacular bereavement of literature" (300). For Nora, it is the very acceleration of history that compels us to preserve memory, and the ethnic and marginalized are uniquely responsible for the production of memory among the postmodern ruins of representation. He argues that "a process of interior decolonization has affected ethnic minorities, families, and groups that until now have possessed reserves of memory but little or no historical capital" (284), as African American blacks.[2]

The marked flesh, as Spillers reminds us, "is the concentration of ethnicity" ("Mama's Baby" 67). Ethnicity, particularly in America over the last three or four decades, as various ethnic and racial communities have been self-consciously striving for the political and cultural power of self-naming, can perhaps be understood as a mnemonics that works against metahistorical assimilation. If an assimilationist model mythicizes the suppression of ancestry and posits identity as self-invention, an ethnic model recognizes and honors that which has been—too often violently—suppressed or sacrificed to that model. Thus, the cultural and political project of ethnicity lays an emphasis on descent over consent, in Werner Sollors's terms (6). Yet, at the same time, contemporary ethnicity, a product of the civil rights campaigns of the sixties, refuses to accept unflinchingly that one's communal location is an inevitable product of historical destiny. Rather it is by excavating the suppressed possibilities of a past that has been erased, by conversing with those ancestral ghosts that lay claim on us, that we can begin, again, to participate in the processes of ethnic self-determination. The past, which has been either denied or utilized as a means of imprisoning us can begin to function as a haunted place, a place through which we begin to imagine a future.

For Morrison, this is not simply a tale of reconciliation, of "overcoming" the violence that defines black history. The critic Deborah Guth summarizes:

> Morrison's novels are themselves acts of repetition both as remembering and transformation. Her extensive use of myth and folk belief to explore the meaning of the present, the open musical architecture of her

work, the oral/aural narrative voice and communal storytelling techniques she deploys all show the degree to which she herself draws upon the past. More important, they dramatize the act of imaginative transformation so central to her thought—the possibility of recreating various traditional forms within a modern, in this case narrative context. On a broader level, of course, the very composition of *Beloved* shows this capacity not simply to "repeat" the past, but to actually transform the chaos of history into a fable of love and bereavement. (590)

A fable of love and bereavement, a mesh of voices that we can find ways to dwell in and between. Morrison's fiction is historical, but, given the urgency of American ghosts, we can—we must—read it as contemporary writing in this way.

It is dangerous for me to invoke Morrison as if she were "representative"; nonetheless, as a general proposition, it seems to me that the clarification of who we are in society—and who me might have been and still may be—by finding ways of speaking to and through the dead, by inventing alternative possibilities out of silence itself, rather than the continued elaboration of a myth of flight and escape, is one crucial aspect of the way in which contemporary fiction participates in the ongoing arguments over the shape and possibility of multiculturalism.

The work of successfully mourning this past and so moving toward an effective recovery, as Brogan confesses, is often incomplete in contemporary ghost stories. And so it is; moreover, though I would underline the participatory, ethical imperative of Brogan's reading of such works, the scheme that would enlist the gothic dimensions of trauma into such utopias (e.g., recovery, health, reintegration) remains a little too pat. For if this is the case, why does Morrison conclude *Beloved* with the extremely ambivalent injunction "this is not a story to pass on" (275)? Insofar as the novel remains enmeshed in bad hauntings, insofar as Sethe remains devoured by her past, so I will argue, do we (certainly in a time when American race relations remain antagonistic, and especially when the ferocity of this historical legacy is publicly disavowed in the name of a new purportedly "postracial" society). That is, in my readings of contemporary gothic, I want to accentuate that which (in Morrison and other writers) eludes the rather naïve narrative of recovery (a psychological model that, after all, hearkens to the discourse of assimilation that many of the works I will examine pointedly resist). As, Richard Burlage, one of the characters in Lee Smith's *Oral History*, puts it, "nothing is ever over, nothing is ever ended, and worlds open up within the world we know"

(229). In the books I explore, ghosts refuse to be fully assimilated, evade the boundaries of generic resolution, and gothic deploys charges and elements that cannot fully be accommodated within any narrative boundaries. They demand more: justice, we might say, an impossibility that everywhere trumps recovery.

Ghost Stories as Cultural Gatekeeping: Lee Smith's *Oral History*

I dwell briefly with Smith's remarkable 1983 Appalachian family saga, *Oral History,* to further elucidate a few of my points. In this novel, composed as a series of tales told by multiple characters and from various points of view, storytelling works as a collective cultural enterprise, cultivated over several generations and serving matriarchal power, designed to police and regulate borders, to negotiate who will be allowed in and who will be excluded from a largely preliterate community in the remote and inaccessible Virginia highlands.[3] "For I am what they call a 'foreigner,'" Burlage notes. "As they use it, this term does not refer to someone from another country, or even from another state, but simply to anybody who was not born in this area of the county. Their insularity astounds" (125). Burlage is an outsider, from the state capital, Richmond, a rationalist and an intellectual on the surface, but a wounded romantic, even a hysteric—he may suffer from what would be today diagnosed as bipolar disorder—and a bit of a fool. Spurned by his upper crust fiancée, suffering, he notes, from a personal malaise and a sense of general decadence in the years after the first world war, he comes to the mountains to teach school and winds up falling in love with Dory Cantrell, the sister of one of his prize students. Hoot Owl Holler, where the Cantrells live and cook up corn liquor, is reputedly haunted, and the tales of haunting serve as one among many mechanisms to repel foreigners. When he journeys to visit the Cantrells, he is greeted by Dory's half-sister, Ora Mae, who "cast her apron up over her head and emitted three loud piercing shrieks" (126). Burlage's colleague, the Reverend Aldous Rife, informs him that "Ora Mae's crying out—those three shrieks—are the universal indicator for 'foreigners' in these mountains, a known sign meant to convey to moonshiners (blockaders, they are termed here) that a stranger is on the way" (132). Rife, who is himself only half-assimilated to mountain life, likewise tries to caution Burlage off by telling him stories of incredible violence. "Is that true?" Burlage demands, after one particularly hair-raising tale; "When was this?"

> "Twenty, thirty years ago," he said. "The time doesn't really matter."
> "Of course it matters. This could be a fact of history, or it could be

a country myth, a folk tale," I said. "I know you collect them, and you
know it too. I suspect you make some of them up."

   "It doesn't matter," he said. "Nothing ever changes that much." (151)

What Burlage misses, and will continue to miss throughout the novel, is that
the veracity of such folk tales is entirely beside the point; rather than recording events accurately, such storytelling constitutes a kind of complex social
technology to regulate community, to secure the rights and legitimacy of
community insiders, and to effectively repel foreigners.

   Indeed, the tale of the haunting, the curse laid upon Hoot Owl Holler, is
initially reported—or more probably, invented—by the first main speaker
in the novel, Granny Younger. Younger is a midwife, a healer, and matriarch
for the community, who recounts how Almarine Cantrell reappears in Hoot
Owl Holler, claims his land, and shacks up with the witch, Red Emmy. Significantly, Granny Younger alerts her audience to the function of storytelling itself: "I'll tell you a story that's truer than true, and nothing so true is
so pretty. It's blood on the moon, as I said. The way I tell a story is the way I
want to, and iffen you mislike it, you don't have to hear" (36). We know that
Granny plays fast and loose with the facts. Almarine was born in 1876, according to the Cantrell genealogy provided by Smith. Yet, Granny insists, he
is only twenty-two in August 1902, the year her tale begins. The "truer than
true" story is the story of the exiling of Red Emmy, whom Almarine, exhausted
near to death by her night-riding and witchery, has to run off. Subsequently,
he marries Pricey Jane, a foreigner whom the elders of the community nonetheless decide to admit; Pricey Jane is later poisoned and dies, and Almarine,
grief-stricken, presumably hunts down and kills Red Emmy. Such is the beginning of the curse on the haunted Hoot Owl Holler.

   Yet, it was Granny Younger herself who insisted to Almarine that Emmy
is a witch, and we are given no other evidence that this is the case, apart from
Granny's slanders. Granny Younger tells what she wants to, she warns us, and
what she wants, it seems, is to drive off a potential rival. As a healer, Younger
is threatened by Emmy's powers; as a claimant to rights over Alamarine's
body and his story, she is sexually threatened by Red Emmy's allure. *Oral
History* is, after all, a series of tales driven by women's sexual jealousy; further, Smith everywhere highlights the link between women's sexual power
and storytelling. Later in the novel, another gifted speaker, Sally, lays claim
to her own rights to speak on behalf of the Cantrells: "There's two things I
like to do better than anything else in the world, even at my age—and one of
them is talk. You all can guess what the other one is" (233). Like Sally, Granny
Younger transforms her erotic energies into the gift of gab. Too old to claim

Almarine sexually, she claims him, rather, by telling him stories designed to make him suspicious of Emmy, and, ultimately, by telling his story. "I knowed what was happening, of course. A witch will ride a man in the night while he sleeps, she'll ride him to death if she can. She can't help it, it is her nature to do so" (53). The sexual rivalry between the Emmy and Granny is pointedly dramatized. Granny ascends the mountain during a thunderstorm and watches the two lovers enviously: "you never saw such kissing in all your life! Made me feel like I had not felt for years and if that surprises you, you ain't got no sense. Now a person mought get old, and their body mought go on them, but that thing does not wear out. No it don't" (52). And Emmy takes the opportunity to signal to Granny that she, Emmy, has won their sexual competition:

> Well, I never said a word, but when they passed by where I was, Red Emmy done something made me see she had knowed I was there all along. Of course she knowed it! Child of the Devil. But I had like to forgot it, that day.
>
> Red Emmy turned her head away from her kissing one time, once only, and looked at me directly where I was hid. The lightning flashes right then and I see her face and it is old, old. It is older and meanern time. Red Emmy stares me right in the eye and she spits one time on the rainy ground. Almarine never seed a thing. (52)

So, Granny takes steps to dispatch Red Emmy, convincing Almarine to banish her and her child: "'You get rid of her, Almarine,' what I told him, 'afore you get a passel of witch children up there'" (55). And, with the help of another village elder, she ensures that he marries the right woman, Pricey Jane, whom, Granny insists, "weren't a foreigner neither, or leastways not as much of one as them others was, her having lived most of her life around Matewan" (63). Thus is the social order preserved and handed down in the tale Granny gives us.

Red Emmy, a symbol of women's sexual agency and erotic power, is never given a chance to recount her story in her own voice. What Granny has effectively repressed from the story is precisely women's desire, and the capacity for that desire to freely express itself. Yet, Emmy, we are told, lays a curse on Hoot Owl Holler, which in the generations to come, is reputed to be haunted. It is haunted, precisely, by a too often repressed women's desire, and the remaining stories, taking place over the next few generations, tell interlinked stories of women's sexual competitions. When Pricey Jane dies, for example, Rose Hibbits moves in to care for him, but her amorous hopes are shattered when she is in turn displaced by Vashti, an "Indian" woman who appears on

Almarine's doorstep with her child, Ora Mae, and who claims to be the wife of Almarine's dead brother. Repulsed, Rose continues to spread untrue rumors:

> "Hit ain't my fault atall. He ast me stay but I won't," I said. "He ast me to get married and I turned him down. Hit's a curse on the whole holler," I said, "and I ain't having any part of it. Almarine has done told me hisself. That witch, she put it on him before he kilt her, and I ain't staying there, Mama, you couldn't pay me to stay." These words come out of my mouth just as smooth as glass, and I liked to have died when I heard them. I had never knowed what I would say till I opened my mouth.
>   "That holler is haunted," I said. (87)

Later, it is Ora Mae, in her envy, who conspires to ruin the relationship between Richard Burlage and Dory, ensuring that Dory will not accompany him back to Richmond. Dory later commits suicide. Thus, in her perceptive reading of the novel, Sonya Smith Burchell points out that "the problem for both [Red Emmy and Dory] is that they exist outside of the community's vision of conformity and acceptable behavior" (112). Finally, it is Pearl, in envy of her sister Sally's sexual freedoms, who leaves Hoot Owl Holler, marries, and becomes a teacher, but who ends up having a scandalous affair with one of her high school students. When Pearl dies in childbirth, along with her infant, her young lover returns to the Holler and murders their brother Billy while he sits rocking, and Billy's ghost continues to haunt the family homestead. Apart from Sally, who leaves the mountains and then returns, who thereby is able to negotiate effectively between the insular community and the outside "foreign world," who reconciles her sexual energy with her capacity for storytelling and thereby assumes the place of Granny Younger as oral historian, we are left with a long string of corpses, the corpses of passionate women, whose unfulfilled passion continues to haunt.

In Smith's fiction, Appalachian storytelling, thereby, is a social mechanism that polices the limits of the culture precisely by policing women's sexuality. Such social structures are as old as patriarchy, of course, and come as no surprise. What might be surprising is that, in this novel, it is women's voices that speak. Although most of the sexually powerful women are silenced—Red Emmy, Dory, and Pearl—other women become authorized to speak. What they *say* turns out both to repress women's sexuality and to acknowledge it: It returns as ghost, as curse. Now, gothic, at its heart, always is structured around a woman's corpse. As the necrophiliac Edgar Allan Poe asserts famously in "The Philosophy of Composition," "the death of a beautiful young woman is unquestionably the most poetical topic in the world" (201). Mute, inacces-

sible, damned, woman's frustrated desire haunts *Oral History,* a chronicle of
a culture, ostensibly patriarchal, where women struggle, through the force of
gossip, medical power, and ritual, to reassert their domain as cultural keepers,
as Brogan indicates, pointing to their restrictive "roles as bearers of culture"
(25). Smith notes, in a reader's guide appended to the Ballantine edition of
the novel, that she views the singer, fiddler, and dulcimer player, Little Luther
Wade, Dory's (and later Ora Mae's) eventual husband, as the ideal folk artist.
Along with bawdy songs of his own composition, Luther sings compositions
that are best described as Hillbilly gothic: "Down in the Valley," "Saint James
Infirmary Blues," "Wildwood Flower," "Barbry Ellen." Typically, these songs
speak of heartbreak, and often of the death of a young woman, who either
commits suicide when abandoned by her lover, or in some cases, is murdered
by the lover because of her roving eye. Smith prefaces the book with the first
two stanzas of the classic folk song, "Fair and Tender Ladies": "If I'd a-knowed
afore I courted / That love, it was such a killin' crime, I'd a locked my heart in
a box of golden / and tied it up with a silver twine." That woman's heart, that
love, locked in the golden casket, is the precise ghost that haunts and ener-
gizes the varying and interlocking speeches of the novel, even if, ultimately,
it remains inaccessible: Red Emmy never speaks. Luther, who speaks of her,
who speaks on her behalf, will ultimately (Smith assures us) be recorded by
Alan Lomax and achieve posthumous renown.

In contradistinction to Luther's indigenous folk art, Richard Burlage, who
begins with literary ambitions but winds up a photographer, represents a nar-
cissistic art, a documentation style that always misses its subject, reflecting,
rather, nothing more than a vainglorious ego of the artist himself. In his pro-
fession, Burlage is modeled after Walker Evans, Dorothea Lange, and other
documentary photographers who chronicled the lives of the impoverished
during the Great Depression. Like Evans's colleague, James Agee, he struggles
ethically to come to grips with his role as "spy." Ultimately, as Agee asserts,
photography fails.[4] Just as Burlage is prevented (and self-prevented) from
gaining an insider's knowledge of the language and manners of the mountains, so too do his photographs miss the essential. When, in 1934, he returns to the mountains, he is interested in nothing so much as the fine figure
he cuts. In the midst of poverty and the depravations occasioned by the coal
mining and timber companies, Burlage drives a fancy car, wears an elegant
hat, and an English scarf, which he adjusts in the mirror of his Packard: "And
the mirror pleased me because of its frame, the way it entrapped my image
and framed it so nicely, reassuring me again that here was a new man, a con-
fident man, so different from the boy who had left here ten years back" (217).
He is, in fact, not so unrecognizable as he would hope, for his old landlady

recognizes him immediately. He takes a series of pictures of the land and the people, "framing everything" (222): "I confess I leaped for my magnifying glass, when upon development, those girls emerged! They were quite a shock to me, validating somehow my theory of photography, if not of life itself: the way a frame can illumine and enlarge one's vision rather than limit it. Frankly, I find in this theory an apologia for the settled life, for the lovely woman I have married who manages things so well yet understands the worth of my artistic pursuits" (223). The picture frame, it turns out, is nothing more than a mirror, which reflects the glory of the artist. The women he photographs represent nothing more than a validation of his own ideas, just as his wife has no other purpose in life than glorifying her man. Wherever Burlage looks, and whatever he shoots, he sees only himself. Ironically, he does not recognize his own children, the twins he has fathered with Dory, and it comes as no surprise that, when he attempts to photograph her from a distance, her visage is blurred:

> But these pictures did not turn out because the light had gone by then! Because Dory, at the door, picked just that moment to turn her head. She was reduced to an indistinct stooped shape, the posture of an older woman—they age so fast in the mountains anyway—or perhaps it was simply the angle of her head and the way she stood at the door, her head a mere bright blur.
> Even when I blew it up, there was nothing there.

In such shots, Dory remains nothing more than an ectoplasmic blur. Even when a passerby, after lecturing Burlage on the economics of hard times, smashes his rearview mirror, Burlage never gets the message. Teacher, man of wealth, man of letters, professional photographer—like Schoolteacher in Morrison's novel, he represents cultural power and authority, and works actively and incessantly to deny his subjects the power to speak on their own behalf.

Which is why, to be sure, such an *oral history,* a tale told from the inside of Appalachia, is, for Smith, so necessary. In Brogan's words, ghosts "figure prominently wherever people must reconceive a fragmented, partially obliterated history, looking to a newly imagined past to redefine themselves for the future" (18). And yet, I am skeptical of the novel's resolution, skeptical as to whether the book successfully manages to effectuate a cultural renewal of a culture that has been ghosted, has been eclipsed by the accelerating forces of change and modernity. In *Oral History,* it remains an open question whether that redefinition for and of the future, however profitable it turns out to be, is successful. For the oral history, the multiple narrative voices honored and quoted so generously within the novel, is itself framed, with great irony. The frame that opens and closes the book is written from the perspective of Jennifer, Pearl's daughter (but, unlike most of the rest of the book, not recounted in the first person). Jennifer, who has been raised by her father after Pearl's affair, has lived a spoiled and sheltered life in the city and returns to investigate her mother's family in the hills. Like Burlage, then, Jennifer is an outsider, a sentimentalist, who sees merely the stereotypes of the people she meets, be they positive—the "salt the earth" (16) she terms her family, when she first meets them, "picturesque" (18)—or negative: "they are really very primitive people, resembling nothing so much as some sort of early tribe. Crude jokes and animal instincts—it's the other side of the pastoral coin" (284). Jennifer, too, has hitched her wagon to the star of cultural authority; she comes to Hoot Owl Holler to complete an assignment for an Oral History course that she is taking at the community college, and, like Dory before her, she has been smitten by her teacher. Like Burlage, in the prose narrative recounting her visit, her style is stilted and self-serving; like Burlage, she will be deliberately repelled by Ora Mae and the other Cantrells—only Little Luther is welcoming to her. Like Burlage, she records her impressions mechanically, leaving a tape recorder in the haunted house to record the sounds of the ghost. Like Burlage, ultimately, Jennifer is incapable of *seeing* anything beyond herself. Ora Mae dismisses her abruptly: "Now you take that thing and you go on. Go on. He never had no business saying you could come on over here in the first place" (282). Ora Mae is talking out now from that place inside her where she knows things. "I reckon you'll find plenty of banging on that tape, everything you want to hear," she says. "You take it and go on, and don't ever come back here no more with no tape recorder because if you set it going up there, you'll likely hear what you don't want to hear" (282). As she leaves, she is sexually assaulted by her cousin, Al, who "grabs her right up off her feet and kisses her so hard that stars smash in front of her eyes. Al sticks his tongue inside her mouth" (285).

Here, in my reckoning, the novel begins, with considerable irony, to turn against itself and to question its own logic. To be sure, Al might be signaling to Jennifer that she is guilty of stereotypical thinking, and there might be a sort of cruel but poetic justice in his deploying what is, after all, the hoariest of Appalachian stereotypes, incest. Yet, we should point out, it is Smith, herself, who deploys the stereotype. At this point, as it concludes, the tense of the novel shifts effectively into the future conditional. Jennifer, we are told, would "never see any of them again" (285). Moreover, the Cantrells, under the patriarchal guidance of the thoroughly modern Al Cantrell, who shares with his namesake and forebear a capacity to prosper, will get rich by capitalizing upon the stereotypes of the haunted house:

> Al will be elected president of the Junior Toastmaster's Club. Then he will make a killing in AmWay and retire from it young, sinking his money in land. He will be a major investor in the ski run which will be built, eventually, on the side of Black Rock Mountain. The success of this enterprise will inspire him to embark on his grandest plan yet: Ghostland, the wildly successful theme park and recreation area (campground, motel, Olympic-size pool, waterslide and gift shop) in Hoot Owl Holler. Ghostland, designed by a Nashville architect, will be the prettiest theme park east of Opryland itself, rides and amusements terraced up and down the steep holler, its skylift zooming up and down from the burial ground where the cafeteria is. And the old homeplace still stands, smack in the middle of Ghostland, untouched. (285)

Again, this is all presented as a hypothetical: It may be Jenny who imagines this future, though it seems outside her fantasy life to predict success for her cousin. The conditional mood, as we have seen, is the place of the specter, of the *might* or *perhaps,* and here, again, we confront the ghost of a dollar. One way or another, Smith is ironizing the manner in which the stereotype lends itself to commodification and becomes a source of profit. In her own way, then, Smith is herself taking on the role of Granny Younger: regulating admittance to the ghost world. And we can't be sure, ultimately, if the novel charts a trajectory from bad to good haunting, even as the past, largely obliterated and inaccessible, is recovered. Certainly, the book endorses an indigenous, and deeply gothic, aesthetic, a story told from the inside. Yet, in alerting us to the financial negations that are a part of delivering that story to the outside, Smith warns us that all such work, her own novel included, risk becoming simply entertainment, simply Ghostland, which commodifies and profits from the very culture it both parodies and exploits.[5]

Trickified Business: Toni Cade Bambara's *The Salt Eaters*

In an important essay on contemporary ethnic writing, Cordelia Chávez-Candelaria defines the "discourse of ethnopoetics" as describing the "process of memorializing through literature and other art forms the varieties of ethnoracial experience and identity":

Ethnopoetic writers and artists locate the conscious struggle to locate
and preserve an ethnic-specific consciousness in the face of a dominant society's dominating language, conventions, and ubiquitous culture. Ethnopoets seek to locate their re/constructions (i.e., imagined
configurations) of an aboriginal cultural past in the present tense of
narrative discourse by foregrounding race, ethnicity, and notions of
primordiality as explicit elements of literature and art. Concerned with
reuniting the ruptured parts of culture perceived and imagined as a
whole, . . . these works share the ethnopoetic preoccupation with ethnoracial identity, yearning for community, and imaginings of an origi-
nary primordial source. (192–193)

In many cases and in other contexts than Appalachian highlands, traditional
ghost stories are mechanisms for enforcing and maintaining power relations
through terror. Geraldine Smith-Wright, for example, has pointed out how,
in the American South, "supernatural tales created by slave owners were specifically designed to capitalize on slaves' worst fears. . . . To press their ad-
vantage, whites often disguised themselves as ghosts, donning white sheets,
walking on stilts, and using tin cans as noisemakers to create mayhem near
the slave quarters—tactics that would later become mainstays of the official
Ku Klux Klan" (143). But such tactics of guardianship are not always effective, she notes, for slaves habitually lived with ghosts: "In the transplanted
African community, among the most important traditions was slaves' strong
conviction that the spirit world was an integral part of the life force. In African traditions regarding the supernatural, the living and the dead are intimately connected, this relationship often taking the form of ancestor wor-
ship. For Africans, it is essential to be on good terms with ancestral spirits. In
fact, deceased family members are considered part of the present family unit"
(144). Ghosts raise the specter of black-white power relations, Smith-Wright
argues, but also provide an opportunity for blacks to turn the tables on white
power. Exploring the rich and highly contested tradition of ghostly folktales
in West African culture and the American South, Smith-Wright asserts that,
in the hands of such black women writers as Toni Morrison and Paule Marshall, ghosts are consequently used to "develop mythic explorations of ways
for culturally disenfranchised Black characters both to acknowledge their
heritage and to forge more satisfying connections with their communities"
(146). As counterpoint, and to conclude this chapter, we can turn to a writer
whose work invokes the supernatural to effectuate an avowed and quite literal "healing" and recovery. Toni Cade Bambara's essential and difficult 1980
novel, *The Salt Eaters,* a book saturated, as Jon Edgar Wideman points out in

the *New York Times Book Review,* by "the nonlinear sacred space and sacred time of traditional African religion—the realm of the Great Time, in which man lives both on the earth and in the presence of his gods" (14). Or, as Gloria Hull points out in her indispensable guide to the novel, "undergirding this emphasis on spiritual unification is TCB's belief (shared by geniuses and mystics) that all knowledge systems are really one system and that 'everything is everything,' that the traditional systems are artificial and merely provide the means for alienating schisms. This basic epistemology is one reason why *The Salt Eaters* is such a 'heavy' book" (130).

The Salt Eaters tells of a spiritual healing undergone by Velma Henry, who has attempted suicide and is now under the care of the healer, Minnie Ransom. Indeed, the very "plot" of the novel involves little more than the two women, seated on stools across from one another in the Southwest Community Infirmary "established in 1871 by the Free Coloreds of Claybourne" (120), Georgia, as Velma finds first that her scars melt away, and her soul is patched together. Albeit a story of healing, the novel complicates the traditional narrative strategy by which the protagonist comes to some insight over her place in the world and awakens to a newfound sense of understanding and/or agency. The book opens by foregrounding the question of desire: "Are you sure, sweetheart, that you want to be well?" (3). Yet Velma's struggle is not the only story being told, as the book rather accompanies various other characters who circle about Claybourne. Bambara is highlighting the intensely social and intersubjective nature of identity, obviously: Velma's story, her identity, is never entirely her own, but is part and parcel of her family, her community, a community that extends back into the past as well as into the future. Consequently, Velma has erred in her isolation. Her godmother, M'Dear Sophie Heywood, rebukes Velma: "And did you think your life is yours alone to do with as you please? That I, your folks, your family, and all who care for you have no say-so in the matter? Whop!" (148). As Margot Anne Kelley points out, "time in these chapters dilates to maintain an overall sense of simultaneity among the events described. In fact, the nearly three hundred page text 'occurs' in only about an hour" (488). Each of the characters, whose thoughts and movements are seemingly aimless or wayward, is an active participant in the elaborate ritual of healing. So too, it seems are the nonevents that haunt the story.

For the fractures in Velma's consciousness are replicated in a fractured community. Bambara wrote the book, she notes, "when I was trying to figure out as a community worker why political folk were so distant from the spiritual community—clairvoyants, mediums, those kind of folks, whom I was always studying with. I wondered what would happen if we could bring them together" (*Deep Sightings* 234–35). In the novel, Velma's husband, Obie, who runs the Academy of the 7 Arts, sits in the gym, one shoe off and one shoe on, and struggles with his awareness of the same split: "And the two major camps, the ones she'd held together, urging each to teach the other its language, had sprung apart. The one argued relentlessly now for the Academy to change its name from 7 Arts to Spirithood Arts and to revamp the program, strip it of material and mundane concerns like race, class and struggle. The other wanted 'the flowing ones' thrown out and more posters of Lenin, Malcolm, Bessie Smith and Coltrane put up" (92–93). Such fissures are as personal as they are political, as much spiritual as physical, Obie realizes: "Maybe the cracking had begun years earlier, when the womb had bled, when the walls had dropped away and the baby was flushed out" (94). And Velma had "found a home among the community workers who called themselves 'political.' And she had found a home amongst the workers who called themselves 'psychically adept.' But somehow she'd fallen into the chasm that divided the two camps" (147). The historical moment of the novel is what Bambara terms "the last quarter"—"of the moon, of the century, of some damn basketball game?" wonders Velma—when "anything can happen. And will" (6). The late 1970s marked the exhaustion of the political movement and, even as early as the Carter years, the dawn of what would be known as Reaganism. "Malcolm gone, King gone, Fanni Lou gone, Angela quiet, the movement splintered, enclaves unconnected. Everybody off into the Maharaji This and the Right Reverend That. If it isn't some far-off religious nuttery, it's some other worldly stuff" (192), laments Velma's friend, Ruby.

"Don't they know we on the rise? That our time is now?" asks Minnie of her spirit guide. "Here we are in the last quarter and how we gonna pull it all together and claim the new age in our name? How we gonna rescue this planet from them radioactive mutants?" (46). The struggle for renewal charted by this novel will consequently enlist the armies of the dead, enlist memory, enlist "many of the old-timers, veterans of the incessant war—Garveyites, Southern Tenant Associates, trade unionists, Party members, pan-Africanists—remembering night riders and day traitors and the cocking of guns"(15), enlist the uncommitted such as Doctor Julius Meadows, a suspiciously light-skinned out-of-towner, who wanders the city, looking for camaraderie, looking to reconnect with his own racial past. It will enlist too the generations of the future, such as Nadeen's unborn child, who leaps in her womb as she witnesses the scars on Velma's wrists fade way, "like the baby Jesus leapt when Elizabeth, big with John, saluted Mary" (111). It will enlist the possibility of a better future, and the options of choices not taken in the past. Much of the novel takes place in the conditional, marked by the repetition of the term *might:* "I might have died" (267), recognizes Velma, as the desire to live is reawakened in her. "She might have died. Might have been struck by the lightning where she sat. But she might have died an infant gasping, but for M'Dear Sophie's holding hands. Might have drowned in her baptism gown" (271). This *might have* too is a kind of ghosting, the haunting of what exists by the alternate paths, the choices not taken, and these alternative futures too fully inform the present and must be honored and recognized as such. That is, for Velma to desire life, she must recognize the *might have* that is her own death. At every crossroads, at every juncture, we choose life or death, and the life we continue to live is honored by the death we have, with the intercession of the gods, avoided. In this sense, too, life is haunted. Earlier, in one of the more confusing passages of the novel, the bus driver, Fred Holt, overcome by chagrin, loneliness, and despair, considers hurtling his bus over the guard rail into the salt marshes outside town, the marshes in which Velma delves, in her memory and in her out-of-body healing, symbolic of death and rebirth. He refrains, and yet one episode of the book dwells on the *might have,* had he done so:

> They might've been twenty seven miles back in the moment of another time when Fred Holt did ram the bus through the railing and rode it into the marshes, stirring bacteria and blue-green algae to remember they were the earliest forms of life and life was beginning again. In the sinking bus trying to understand what happened, was happening, would happen and stock still but for the straining for high thoughts to buoy them all up. But sinking into the marshes thick with debris and intrusion. Faces frozen at the glass seeing with two eyes merely the onlookers on the embankment holding their breath, or seeing closer by with two eyes the bullfrogs holding theirs in the shallows, the dragonflies suspended over the deeps and the wind waiting, the waters still and waveless till the shock of the plunge registered and the marshes sucked thing sunder. (86–87)

What happens, instead, is a "sonic boom" (87). At each juncture in the novel where death and life confront one another, the apocalypse is marked by this thundering, which is variously interpreted as thunder, as trains, as drumming. So too will renewal involve the intercession of the loa, who arrive via bus in Claybourne, and whose thunderings, variously overheard in the novel and mistaken for trains, thunder, drums, will, like Papa Legba, stand at the crossroads and open the door into the future. Minnie, for example, gets into a long series of quarrels with her spirit guide, Old Wife, about other haints,

Chapter 2

Christianity, and voodoo. "I'm talking about them haints that're always up to some trickified business. They ride busses just the same's they ride brooms, peoples, carnival floats, whatever. All the same to them. What they care about scarin people with they ghostly selves?" (43). Old Wife can't tolerate haints, though she is a haint herself:

> "Old Wife, what are you but a haint?" Minnie asks:
> "I'm a servant of the Lord, beggin your pardon."
> "I know that. But you a haint. You dead, ain't you?"
> "There is no death in spirit, Min, I keep tellin you. Why you so hard head?" (62)

Ultimately, the moment will come that will spin the world off its axis: "No one remarked on any of this or on any of the other remarkable things each sensed but had no habit of language for, though felt often and deeply, privately. That moment of correspondence—phenomena, noumena—when the glimpse of the life script is called dream, déjà vu, clairvoyance, intuition, hysteria, hunger, or called nothing at all" (89). "That was the kind of thunderbolt that knocked Saul off his steed and turned him into Paul," remarks Cora Rider (278). This is the moment, where "something happened" to Fred Holt, where Obie is "stripped by lightning" and awakes to salute "the future, gold splashing in his eyes" (292). This is the moment that will redeem, that will, ultimately, transform the world and renew it.[6] As the novel concludes, as Velma emerges from her "burst cocoon" (295), the novel points to a provisional future, not, Velma will realize, to an end to the struggle, but even so, to hope.

Atlanta Gothic: Writing the Atlanta Child Murders

Bambara's concerns are ever at and with these crossroads, between suffering and survival, between an acute sensitivity to the physical burdens of historical suffering and the inevitable necessity of paradoxical and hard-won optimism, between the political work that drives her characters and the spiritual solace they need to muster in order to sustain such efforts, and, of course, with the historical crossroads of post–civil rights America. In her novels and films, Bambara aims to diagram and envision "a reconceptualization of 'America' and a shift in the power configurations of the USA" (*Deep Sightings* 178). Clearly, the political, social, and geographic racial reconfiguration of the United States, for better *and* (in certain respects) for worse, marks the most significant change in the country over the last few decades of the twentieth century.

Peter K. Eisinger of the Institute for Research on Poverty at the University of Wisconsin published a book in 1980 entitled *The Politics of Displacement: Racial and Ethnic Transition in Three American Cities.* The study analyzes the process of black municipal empowerment in Detroit and Atlanta, certified by the mayoral elections of Coleman Young in 1973 and Maynard Jackson in 1974. In his preface, Eisinger writes that "contrary to general expectations, the transition to black rule in Atlanta and Detroit has been remarkably benign. Neither city seems to be dying in any sense. For the most part, white resources have neither withdrawn nor turned to opposition. The politics of these cities, at least into 1979, have been marked not by racial conflict but by patterns of coalition-building, cooperation, and accommodation that crossed the deep racial divide" (xxi). Though he leaves open the question of whether "the increases in political power achieved by black elites" will "lead gradually to economic gains for the black masses" (xviii), Eisinger saw reason for a "certain optimism," measured against "the history of race relations in those two cities, . . . the habits of racial oppression in American society, and . . . a virtually worldwide tendency to deal with ethnoracial political competition by violent means" (xxi).

From a vantage point nearly thirty years on, at a moment when the political ascendancy of African Americans has been so surprisingly expanded to the federal domain, it seems clear enough that Eisinger's optimism was, nonetheless, in many respects misplaced. Detroit is certifiably dead, a victim of Rust Belt deindustrialization and the flight of white capital.[7] Atlanta is a more complicated case; the municipality is proud to acknowledge itself one of the great winners of the world system of deregulated global capitalism, since the abandonment of the Bretton Woods system of monetary regulation in the mid 1970s. As a quick glance at Wikipedia will tell you, Atlanta is designated a Gamma World City and is a financial giant, home to many Fortune 1000 companies. Approximately 60 percent of the population is African American, and Atlanta has been governed by black mayors since 1973. Yet, financial power was fleeing from the center; as the commentator on contemporary urban American, James Howard Kunstler writes in his satiric take on the city: "Atlanta was doing what every other place in the country wished it could do, and in spades, producing unprecedented new wealth and prosperity. Atlanta was becoming a collection of fabulous Edge Cities, which, the cognoscenti would tell you, was what the future would be all about—brilliant sparkling satellite pods of corporate high-rise dynamism embedded in a wonderful matrix of leafy, tranquil dormitory suburbs, all tied together by a marvelously efficient transportation system" (45).

However, the *displaced* in Eisinger's title refers not to those left behind in the city's core, but rather to white elites who surrendered political control of the city to black politicians. Yet a much greater displacement occurs in the transition to the new economy. One-quarter of the population lives below the poverty line, and the number is significantly higher among the young and the elderly. A focus on the relative tranquility of the transition itself displaces the violence of economic injustice. More pointedly, we should recall, violent racial conflict persists: The string of killings that have become known as the Atlanta Child Murders were occurring at the very time the study was published. As Jeff Prugh, the investigative journalist who, with Chet Dettlinger, penned *The List* (1984), an account which questions the official storyline and the verdict, points out, "it is one of the most reported, but least told, stories of our times" (5). "And," Toni Cade Bambara adds, "until a Black man was collared, it was unacceptable to speak of hate" (19).

Moving, then, from the southern small town of Claybourne to the contemporary urban metropolis, and taking as its pretext Toni Cade Bambara's remarkable posthumously published (1999) novel, *Those Bones Are Not My Child*, a fictionalized depiction of the Atlanta Child Murders of 1979–81, this section couples the problems of contemporary gothic and ghosts with urban violence, race, communal and familial trauma, documentary fiction, the "new south" and the reformation of urban life, and contested memories, official and otherwise. Though Wayne Williams was convicted in 1982 for two of the murders, former DeKalb County police chief Louis Graham was convinced (as are many in Atlanta) that Williams, as he maintains, was innocent and launched a cold case investigation that lasted from 2005 to 2007 (apparently turning up no significant new evidence). The dissatisfaction with the Williams's verdict, however, runs deeper than debates about his particular guilt or innocence and stems, according to Bambara, largely from the way in which the official "closing" of the case overcodes, dominates, and silences alternative possibilities. The arrest certified the story that official Atlanta told of itself to the world and muted the myriad ways of knowing practiced by its denizens: "media was unaware—or rather, made uninterested in the fact— that there were numerous other bodies of investigators conducting inquiries and coming up with findings more plausible than the explanations offered by the Task Force" (18). Thus the official "cover-up" in Williams's arrest and conviction camouflages not only the fact that he was indicted for only two murders, of adults rather than of the official twenty-nine (and many more, unofficially) children murdered, and circumspectly avoids the possibility of Klan or other forms of white involvement (e.g., sadomasochistic porn rings, high-level government conspiracy). More urgently, the cover-up judicially mutes and suppresses the Atlanta black community's agency in unraveling the crimes and participating actively in their own resistance and healing: "As the grapevine sizzled with charges of hate-motivated murder and official cover-up, the authorities made their arrest of a man who in no way resembled any of the descriptions of the Task Force reports, any of the sketched faces pinned to the corkboard in command headquarters. In no way resembled the descriptions in the reports of STOP's independent investigators, or in the reports of community workers investigating well out of the limelight" (7). Thus, as Eric Anderson argues, the novel can be read as a struggle for competing claims, competing narratives over the rights to the story, and the rights to the city. Anderson notes the "rhetoric of novelty" that drives the narrative of the Atlanta Child Murders, a story of black-on-black violence and the success of cutting edge crime-solving techniques by the FBI: "Whose city, whose place, is Atlanta? Whose children are being murdered, and whose are not? Whose communities have been riven, socially and environmentally? Commissioner of Public Safety Lee Brown, the Atlanta police, and the FBI appear to brush off such questions and concerns, while ... Dettlinger and ... Prugh in their true-crime book *The List,* Toni Cade Bambara in *Those Bones Are Not My Child* (1999), and Tayari Jones in *Leaving Atlanta* (2002) try to keep the story open, unresolved, haunting, familiar, and mindful of the ecosocial places of the dead and the living. Such openness is far from easy" (197). Anderson continues: "Instead, she sets out to revise and challenge a variety of prevailing official narratives about the victims, the suspects, the convicted murderer, the contexts, and the consequences of these racialized serial murders. Along the way, she exposes—or reawakens—her readers to what happens at the crossroads of the ecological and the social, the disposable and the renewable, the mundane and the horrific, and she urges a complex, place-based sense of complicity that demonstrates both the ease and the dangers of disengagement" (200).

Murder epidemics, such as the ongoing *feminicidios* in Juarez, Mexico, or the serial slaughter of over 520 aboriginal women in Canada, expose the terrors of encroaching modernization and industrialization that lay siege to deeply rooted patterns of community organization. In Atlanta, "New International City ... Black Mecca of the South. Second Reconstruction City ... Slated to make the Top Ten of the world's great financial centers" (18), Bambara depicts the crisis as embroiling parents of victims and inner-city community organizers in complex contestations with the technocratic and bureaucratic apparatus enlisted to enforce and rationalize emergent financial and social powers. In a nutshell, the novel proceeds by subjecting the "authorized" narratives of the child murders and their putative resolution to a series of interrogations from below, as the silenced speak up: Those who suffer the loss of their children—and indeed, the slaughtered children themselves—insist that their varying experiences and modes of comprehension be heard and addressed. As a corollary, these insurgent voices like those in *The Salt Eaters* everywhere map the historical moment and link their own suffering to the late seventies suppression of revolutionary movements and to the global economic and political disfranchisement of the underclasses.

Bambara is crystal clear that her aesthetic and political task as a writer and filmmaker involves reclaiming the rights to storytelling. She speaks of "assuming the enormous tasks of reconstructing cultural memory, of revitalizing usable traditions of cultural practices, and of resisting the wholesale and unacknowledged appropriation of cultural items—such as music, language, culture, posture—by the industry that then attempts to suppress the roots of it—where it came from—in order to sustain its cultural hegemony" (*Deep Sightings* 141–42). The daunting novel, as Carol Anne Taylor points out, "blurs the parameters of essay, investigative journalism, history (including oral history), epic, tragedy, satire, historical novel, realist novel, metafiction, and more" (259), a list to which we might add, not incidentally, a "whodunit" on a cosmic scale and gothic.

If mystery novels typically offer us a fable of (at least relative) reassurance that the guilty will be found out and punished, gothic, as I have been arguing, provides no such consolation. In gothic works, guilt cannot be fully assigned, and the cosmic and secular operations of justice always remain an open question. Contemporary gothic, as I have been arguing, is a narrative stratagem central to the recapturing of a past that has been fractured and ruptured, sometimes dispensed with, more often deliberately denied to besieged communities, struggling to maintain and reproduce their cultures against the institutions of cultural genocide or under conditions of endocolonization and diaspora. Consequently, the novel itself comes to function as a sort of ossuary of the dismembered and, as Bambara's editor, Toni Morrison, might say, the "disremembered," the unmourned and unclaimed victims of contemporary American urbanization. Ultimately, Bambara's aesthetic tactic will be, as Martyn Bone asserts, "recovering and representing" that which is, literally and figuratively, disposable and disposed of: "Bambara's struggle[s] to make language material enough to represent and dignify the flesh and bones of Atlanta's dead black children" (242)

The novel is framed by a prologue that documents her own political and immediately maternal anxieties; Bambara's concerns in all her work involve motherhood, community, and the eclipse of the revolutionary movements of the 1960s. In *Deep Sightings and Rescue Missions,* she speaks in the wake of the sixties, of "the walking wounded and defectives, not only agent types, but also people who are still stumbling around from the sixties who were never embraced quite enough, who got assigned things to do and then got left hanging and are still walking around blasted" (218). With regard to Atlanta, thus, "community sleuths," she points out,

> clocked federal agents in and out of Atlanta as early as summer 1980. There were feds investigating alleged kidnappings even as the official word to the public and parents was "runaways." But other feds, using the Missing and Murdered cases as a cover, were engaged in COINTELPRO-like operations, particularly against the Revolutionary Communist Party and the Central American Support Committee. President Carter, who made no secret of suspicions and alarm over the dangerously clandestine nature of the intelligence operations, was the one hope clung to by citizens subjected to FBI break-ins routinely blamed on burglars. The election of President Reagan, though, changed the picture. Both the intelligence community and the right-wing insurgents stepped up their covert activities, overseas and on home ground. (20)

Those Bones unfolds through the central consciousness of a mother, Marzala Rawls Spencer (Zala), whose son, Sundiata (Sonny), has disappeared. As Taylor points out, Zala's initial response is to notify the authorities, a tactic that evidently fails as she encounters disbelief, indifference, bureaucratic high-handedness, and offhand racist and sexist dismissal. Torn between bouts of lethargic despair and fits of frenetic activity, Zala will be compelled to league together with an odd grouping of community activists—friends, Vietnam veterans, renegade police officers and technocrats, radical journalists—in order to accelerate the search for her child and reclaim her own flagging and threatened agency.

To do so will involve a necessary remapping of the city and of her own past. A central tension in the book involves the clash between rooted patterns of perception and strategies of understanding and the official cover-up. The conflict between these distinctly opposed epistemologies is dramatized as the distinction between a distant or abstract perspective, on the one hand, and an indigenous, experiential, and historical mode of dwelling in the city, on the other. In his own remarkable reckoning of the murders, *The Evidence of Things Not Seen,* James Baldwin makes the important distinction between "affluence" and "wealth," which "is not the same thing. . . . Wealth, that is, is not the power to buy, but the power to dictate the terms of that so magical marketplace—or at the very least to influence those terms" (38). Further, Bambara insists, the very erasure of links between wealth and production in-

volves a historical secretion of ideological gerrymandering—that is, dispossession—and, as we have seen, the gothic marks the space of financial dispossession. Consequently, the city becomes gothic, disorienting; the spatial
conceit of the novel presents two Atlantas: the Atlanta of affluence on display,
and the Atlanta that has been produced primarily through black labor. Each
is encountered by Zala as she drives the streets, noticing first the "impressive
skyline" seen from afar, "the glass towers, the skyscraper hotels, the banks,
the revolving club lounges on the tops of buildings" (82) and that other Atlanta, witnessed from within:

> Zala had always prided herself on her knowledge of the city; its back
> roads, parks, and campuses; its architecture and monuments, the vari-
> ous ways brickworkers had of signing their buildings; the iron mongers
> who kept African motifs alive without knowing it, the county borders,
> the voting districts that kept shifting their lines since the day Primus
> King cast the first Black ballot down in Columbus, Georgia. Her first
> training had come from her dad, tickled to death with the dollbaby
> born to him and Mama Lovey late, in their middle-age years. He would
> ride her all over the city in the old Ford truck as he replaced down-
> spouts, flushed dormers, cleaned gutters, talked history, and shared his
> professional secrets with her as though the five-year old Zala would
> grow up to be a carpenter, a glazier, a handywoman, or all three. (83)

Further, the book everywhere highlights a network of connections among
personal trauma, the new capitalism, and globalized racial conspiracies: "Wake
up, Africans!" (167), admonishes a speaker in Central City Park, "The U.S.
government is up to no good in Grenada. They're sending infiltrators into Jamaica to bust up the trade union movement. They're down there in Miami
training death squadrons for South American fascists" (168). "And people,
good people, right here in Atlanta, in 'Lovely Atlanta,' someone is killing our
most treasured resource, our most precious people, our future—our children" (171). Zala's estranged husband, Spence, watches a documentary on
television:

> Government by torture. The bullet ridden body of Che Guevara; the
> attacks on the Tupermaro in Uruguay; the overthrow of Allende, the
> forced sterilization of Andean laborers; the wholesale slaughter of the
> Quiche Indians in Guatemala; Argentine Jewry one percent of the popu-
> lation, twenty percent of the disappeared. Strikers in U.S. companies
> in Central and South America disappearing. The Women of the Dis-

appeared petitioning the government, appealing to the populace. Am-
nesty International's statistics. Floggings, chemical zombification, ar-
rests and executions without trial. The interrogated bound and gagged,
suspended from poles, and beaten. Cables plugged into crank-up ra-
dios. Jumper-cable pinchers attached to the nipples. Electric prods slid
past the penis to the anus, then shoved. (175)

Finally, rule by terror and disappearance corresponds to the magical logic
of capitalism, the erasure of the source of profits. As Bone has argued, drawing on the work of Patricia Yaeger on the black "throwaway body" in Southern literature, the book advances a "metaphor of dematerialization" (231) at
the heart of finance capital. *Those Bones Are Not My Child* "reveals how the
hegemony of (finance) capital, even as it defines and shapes the 'international
city,' abstracts the other Atlanta—grimly symbolized and embodied by the
missing and murdered children—out of existence. . . . Bambara constructs a
grotesque body politics of place in order to critique the economic motivation
and definition of 'international' Atlanta, and to refocus our attention upon
the dead and disappeared children. Finally, . . . Bambara also pans out from
this localized vision, centered on the neighborhood and the body, to resituate 'international' Atlanta within a world-system of inequality and exploitation" (230).

In chapter 3, I will return to the discussion of how the genre of contemporary gothic vexes global capitalism. Suffice it to point out here that what we
confront in both of Bambara's novels, given their historical location in the late
1970s and early 1980s, however, is a situation where the older revolutionary
potential of the 1960's movements is not yet dead, and the new world—which
will be either one of untrammeled global inequality and exploitation or one
that might see revolutionary hope acted upon—struggles to be born. Such are
the political and ethical crossroads that define the fourth quarter, the gothic
interregnum—the years between 1968 and 2001. At any rate, the ethnocentric American game, like the American century, is drawing to a close.

Gothic Trauma and the Question of National Recovery

I have so far considered what are to my mind a few key texts, which in short-
hand suggest the ubiquity and diversity of late-twentieth-century gothic. Taken
together, they testify to some genuine concerns about the future of the political and cultural project of America. What will we become over the course of
the twenty-first century? And how have we gotten there? Perceptive readers

may also catch the allusion in my book's title to the posthumous publication of the late Angela Carter, among whose recurrent obsessions were perverse identities glossed over and served up in an American cinematic tradition, not least of which are the ways in which the westerns of John Ford, which sporadically refigure the imperial assignations of a manifest racial destiny as national, foundational epic, encounter the aboriginal continental spirits of "los indios." Carter's "Gun for the Devil" in *American Ghosts and Old World Wonders,* where "the unknown continent, the new world, issues forth its banned demonology" (58), is frontier gothic with a twist, insisting still that, as D. H. Lawrence intimated, "there is too much menace in the landscape" (Lawrence 51); "America hurts," wrote Lawrence, "because it has a powerful disintegrative effect on the white psyche. It is full of grinning, unappeased aboriginal demons, too, ghosts, and it persecutes the white men" (51). Lawrence holds forth the hope, if it can be called that, that these ghosts may, ultimately, be appeased, exorcised, put to final rest through the frontier drama of recuperative violence.[8] Here we can recognize the roots of the typical definition of gothic as espousing a worldview of fundamental terror, and yoking it, for better or for worse, to (white male) paranoia, as is apparent in the postmodern gothic of William Burroughs, say, or Thomas Pynchon, or Denis Johnson in such books as *Already Dead: A California Gothic,* or the films of Quentin Tarantino, David Lynch, or the Coen brothers.[9] For me, however, this formulation will not, not quite, suffice, as the playful subversions of Carter's refiguration of gothic intimate. Terror and paranoia, I believe, are fraternal rather than identical twins, and gothic is the familiar language in which they communicate. Thus Savoy, for example, insists that the "*entire* tradition of American gothic can be conceptualized as the attempt to invoke 'the face of the tenant'—the specter of Otherness that haunts the house of national narrative—in a tropics that locates the traumatic return of the historical preterit in an allegorically preterited mode, a double talk that gazes in terror at what it is compelled to bring forward but cannot explain, that writes what it cannot read" (13–14, my emphasis).

The repetitions and reprisals of trauma, however, are likewise pinioned by history, and wonder, as Carter intimates, may well be as feasible a response to the return of the historically repressed as terror. No doubt the narrative strategies typically deployed by gothic border on the hysterical; the systematic attempts to banish, deny, or exorcise the unruly, thronging ghost or ghosts transmutes into a frenzied attempt to punish or confine the medium or intercessionary. Michele Masse, for example, makes the strong argument that traditional gothic novels involve a complex strategy to police female desire, and as we have seen, there is *always* in gothic the battered, abused, and violated corpse of a woman, a mother, generally displayed as both an object of fascination and as a moral lesson (think of the spectacle of Isabella Rossellini's bruised body in *Blue Velvet*). Yet such containment strategies, outlandish in any case, symptomatically lose the struggle to control desire and confess in their very excess to that surrender, a loss of control satirized, for example, in Charlotte Perkins Gilman's notorious ghost story "The Yellow Wallpaper." Yet gothic will often be seized, as it were, by an exposition of its own futility, and it is the unflagging insistent beckoning of these seizures that we will want—that we will need—more fully to honor. Carter, for her part, makes a virtue of the psychic disintegration of autonomous Anglo-Saxon subjectivities. And for such critics as Gordon and Brogan, as well as Bonnie Winsbro, it is the generous receptivity to the needs and desires of that willful, historically brutalized tenant, a hesitant and troubled hospitality to that unacknowledged Other that marks and defines a new direction in American fiction and culture.

For, in what I term (for reasons that should by now have become clear), the *abortive epic* of American expansion, examples of which range from the Leatherstocking Tales to the Cold War Western cinema, the cultural entombment, the ceremonial purges, and the banishment of ghosts—the ghosts of difference—to their proper place, fails, over and over again. Entombment is a policy of cultural inscription and ascription, pursued through means of Indian removal, for example, as Goddu has demonstrated, along with slavery, genocide, ghettoization, misogyny, a centuries-long effort, as Spillers writes, to "keep difference under wraps" ("Who Cuts the Border?" 9).

Attuned to the oneiric and differential tensions of the fin-de-siècle, Edmundson's *Nightmare on Main Street,* which I began to discuss earlier, is an insightful study of the ubiquity of gothic conventions and sensibilities in contemporary American cultural life. Edmundson delineates the gothic character of everything from Wes Craven's slasher flicks to the O. J. Simpson trial, demonstrating, for example, the ways in which the discourse of addiction has supplanted the older notion of haunting in the vernacular idiom. He even targets so-called post-structuralist thinking; the theories of Derrida and Foucault, for example, are bound up with an irredeemably gothic return of the repressed. They remain self-indulgently haunted, insofar as the metaphysics of presence, in one case, or power, in the other, refuse to give up the ghost, refuse to bury themselves, refuse to yield to new possibilities. Power and difference return, like ghosts, everywhere we turn; they will not be exorcised. For Edmundson, contemporary gothic formations remain largely cynical; that is, if gothic certifies, as I've been arguing, a "present in thrall to the past" (5), it implies that our destiny is to remain mournful prisoners of a past that sa-

distically confines us, without our ever being able to comprehend the reasons for our incarceration. As in William Godwin's gothic political thriller,
Caleb Williams, for example, one of the founding texts of the genre, or any
of Thomas Pynchon's novels, we are dupes of a vast conspiracy, a conspiracy
whose contours mystify even the conspirators. American social and political struggles, according to such a scenario, devolve into a pattern of family
feuds, where neither Hatfields nor McCoys can recall why they are slaugh-
tering one another's family members. As we will never be able to understand
the rationale for a conspiracy (in which we are both victim and perpetrator),
much less outwit it, contemporary gothic counsels us to a profoundly cynical resignation, according to Edmundson's reading. Discussing what he terms
"apocalyptic gothic" in, for example, the deep ecology movement, he emphasizes how hysterical fear-mongering disables political will to action: "It is one
thing to be obsessed by environmental decay, something else to be mesmer-
ized by the fiction of the serial killer as an avenging angel. Yet when the discourses of environmentalism or of AIDS make the Gothic turn, and stay on
that road—when they become formulaic horror stories—the result is pas-
sivity and fear. Motives for political action or for scientific research can disappear beneath waves of Gothic paranoia" (29). As gothic then everywhere
fails to come to grips with the barbaric manifestations of a misguided past
and figures the future as unredeemed catastrophe, it retreats into a postur-
ing, a pouting, which is nothing more than, well, downright reactionary. Witness, for example, the popularity of a writer like Anne Rice, whose preda-
tory, faux-aristocratic vampires are presented as idealized figures of glamour,
role models, almost: "She seems to have sensed the fact that in the age of the
Reagan-Bush plutocracy, readers would be more than happy to throw their
allegiances to the higher orders" (43).

Vampires have, as the *Twilight* films suggest, become increasingly important to young adolescents, marking as they do sexual thresholds to be
crossed; they cannot, however, simply be reduced to emblems of misunder-
stood adolescents. Rice's characters do aspire to a sort of Nietzschean super-
heroism, insofar as they are figures of fantasy, a fantasy of power. However,
Edmundson is correct to align Rice with the gothic of ressentiment (just as
Reagan-Bushism, itself a rather cynical political ploy with no other apparent aim than to rob from the poor and give to the rich, is able—often by deploying gothic imagery—to evoke an apocalyptic dread of minorities to re-
inforce its appeal to the genuine discontent of working-class whites; we can
witness examples of such racial scapegoating at rallies for vice-presidential
candidate Sarah Palin). Gothic then, which allegorizes our terror, fails, in Ed-

mundson's estimation, to offer compelling alternatives to our predicament. The discourse of contemporary gothic, according to Edmundson, is enmeshed in an unconsummated dialectic with techniques of "facile transcendence": for example, the middlebrow aspirations of daytime television shows such as *Oprah;* the array of bogus New Age therapies, offering a cheaply purchased, consumerist "therapeutic sublime" (77); the double-dealing rhetoric of Alcoholics and Narcotics Anonymous—all typified in the insipid shenanigans of *Forrest Gump.* This film, a celebratory triumph of the trivial, simply disarms and discredits the cruelties of the past. Gump, for example, emerges unscathed (and stupendously rich) from his misadventures in Vietnam, and viewers are jokingly asked to identify with the happy-go-lucky Gump; we are never invited to read such lunacies as satire. What we are left with, at the century's turn, in this dialectic is a chiliastic cultural landscape of sterile "impassivity." Americans, then (and Edmundson pointedly fails to interrogate this term), are trapped between their unconsummated dread of a spectral complex it hearkens to but cannot fully engage and a desperately ill-fated fantasy of transcendence that purchases off-the-rack solutions to our implicit unhappiness: shoddy goods.

I will quarrel with, however, and hope to complicate Edmundson's contention that American gothic is destined to be politically debilitating or sterile. His argument is a savvy work of cultural criticism, compelling, seductive, but only insofar as it ventures down Main Street. Other things, other monstrosities, other hauntings, conspire in the back alleys and byways, off the map, we might say, of middle America. In other words, Edmundson's project allies itself with a mainstream version of American liberalism, embracing an assimilationist credo that American hauntings have thoroughly discredited. American haints—and their number, I argue, is legion—are not in the business of reassuring "us" in any way. Again, my point is that these texts are not merely trauma, but gothic; trauma narratives necessarily imply the possibility, at least, of recovery, whereas gothic leaves the question radically open. For Edmundson, the ghosts that haunt the American project must be fully reckoned with (this is the posited task of culture, after all) but only, eventually, to be appeased, to be exorcised. But who wants appeasement? Who wants exorcism? Who wants transcendence? Ghosts speak for a *justice that beggars any act of cultural recovery:* They want more, and more, and still more. To my mind, for example, Edmundson egregiously misreads Morrison's gothic *Beloved,* seeing it as a work that aims at healing, at reintegration, at reconstruction. The book, he claims, fails to make good on the "transcendence" it holds forth: "The Gothic burden isn't so much overcome as it is shifted—the crime of slavery finds its true culprit. But as to how to overcome guilt and shame and the sorry weight of the past through some action in the present, the book offers no conception" (177).

But then why should it? Moreover, it never aims to. As Morrison asserts, the enormity of the crime (sixty million and more, reads the epigraph) suggest that any reintegration, the move to community and the gesture toward love, self-love, in the book's closing chapter, will never be complete. *Beloved* never aspires to be a novel of "healing"—love, after all, is shattered and traumatized, it is never what we might think of as health but engages, fully, the passions of suffering (historical and personal: the two cannot be disentangled, in Morrison's vision). Rather, love—and the book's title carries an injunction, an imperative: "Be Loved!" (because, as the holy woman, Baby Suggs, reminds her congregation of blacks, "they don't love your mouth. *You* got to love it. This is flesh I'm talking about here. Flesh that needs to be loved" [88])—is still a gaming with ghosts; if it is health, if it heals, it is a haunting still, a haunted kind of health.

But to say that reintegration, recovery, is partial or incomplete is not to say it has failed: quite the opposite. We can never let the dead bury their dead, much as we might want to. The dead remain with us, even in their absence, even in their anonymity (this is not, the novel closes, a story to pass on). "Just get over it," Edmundson seems to be saying, "get over it and move on!" Anything else, apparently, would be merely to wallow in shame and grief, as if the process of mourning, of grief, might be brought to "closure." He aspires to a genuine transcendence, examples of which might be found in romantic poetry, as opposed to a facile transcendence. But by the end of his argument, the two look increasingly similar. He closes by echoing the insipid rhetoric of popular healing that he had earlier excoriated.

In chapter 3, I will endeavor to take seriously the implications of Edmundson's apocalyptic gothic. Let me end this chapter here, however, by pointing out that this is because Edmundson's ideal is, finally, integrationist: He is, after all, a dialectician. And the gothic has no use for dialectics, as Edmundson admits in his reading of Marx. Ghosts haunt the borders of whatever syntheses culture might proffer; however genuine or authentic these syntheses, ghosts want more. We might counter his "Gothic" (a term which Edmundson, significantly, always capitalizes), with the radical minor gothic of such a writer as Leslie Marmon Silko, for example. In Silko's ethical spiritualism, an endeavor that is syncretic rather than assimilationist, the armies of the dead want nothing more than the full repossession of the land: Indigenous peoples (and their miscegenated offspring—Silko is no racial purist) demand that Europeans go back to Europe. If assimilation stresses the erasure of difference, the relative integration of minority communities into the mainstream, a syncretic approach is more parasitical. The critic and novelist Louis Owens has stressed the importance of mixed blood metaphors and characters in Native writing, but, following Simon Ortiz, emphasizes "the characteristically Indian creative incorporation of 'foreign ritual, ideas, material in Indian terms'"(*Other Destinies* 168).

Edmundson is on firmer ground (if still haunted ground), nonetheless, when he situates the emergence of contemporary American gothic from the unfinished projects associated with the social and political ferment of the 1960s, although, as I will argue, contemporary gothic, which has many histories, notably refers back to the latter half of the nineteenth century as well: the Civil War and the failures of the Reconstruction, the long sad trajectory of Jim Crow laws, the botched Indian policies. Though he avoids any mention of Bambara's work, this unfinished project is precisely what haunts America. The specters we have been haunted by at the close of the twentieth century arise from the graves of "civil rights, the struggle for women's rights, the gay movement, the youth movement, a sexual rebellion, and a general drive for broad human enfranchisement [which] took off in the period just before and during the Vietnam War" (64). Thus, "it is perhaps not entirely accidental that many '90s Gothic scenarios involve members of these newly insurgent groups in central roles. Our Gothic melodramas teem with transgressor blacks like O. J. Simpson and Michael Jackson; with enraged women like Lorena Bobbitt, Tonya Harding, and the purported victims of once-repressed sexual abuse; and with adolescents and even children in one state or another of sexual abandon. What did this '60s movement to so-called liberation let loose? Has it not, ultimately, led to an age of chaos?" (64) Well, not really, at least not beyond the paranoid dread of conservatives (and Goths, insofar as gothic formations enlist themselves in the conservative movement, as Edmundson asserts they often do).[10]

Such critics as Brogan and Edmundson have, I think, their fingers on the pulse of an American culture, if neither is fully willing to confirm the chiliastic rapacity of the ghosts they find there. Both studiously avoid such difficult writers as Silko, whose works resists such schematic scenarios, not to mention, for instance, the hungrily satirical dimensions of contemporary gothic in the hands of a writer like, say, Gerald Vizenor. Both, I think, are unable to come to grips with the most radical challenges of Bambara, or of Morrison, whose multidimensional works also elude the will to power of such resolved readings; *Beloved* is neither (or only partially) a book of potentially successful recovery; nor does it boil down to reverse racism (although white power in America has never, and still shows no real signs of, effective conciliatory gestures). On the one hand, gothic remains mired in a political debilitating and anxious dread; on the other, it moves us toward an idealized cultural recovery, a productive understanding of who we are, have been, how we have suffered, and who we might be. Either the political work of gothic culture is largely avoided or else it is largely accomplished; in either case, it is understood that the ideal, if not fully assimilationist, at least involves a mutually peaceful and harmonious coexistence between and among minorities and dominant powers. Not a bad goal, all-in-all, but America remains far too savage a place for it to be achievable in any of the terms we have been saddled with (and an institutionalized American savagery, a patently obvious fact of corporate capitalism, is something American cultural commentators for some reason seem unable to acknowledge). I am not being cynical here—quite the opposite. The language of justice, of freedom, of liberation, seems to have been largely exiled from the American rhetorical landscape—or when it appears, does so only in the most cynical of forms. This is glaringly true, especially after September 11, a moment whose fallout looked (and may still look) to have involved for a decade now the most hysterical retrenchment of nationalist clichés. Contemporary gothic, then, arrives as no surprise. Gothic cultural texts do, in many cases, perform or fail to perform in the ways Edmundson and Brogan describe. Edmundson, after all, largely addresses popular culture, a fairly easy target, whose targets have never been famous for moving us to transcendence. Indeed, their diametrically opposed readings of Morrison's novel speak to a possibly gendered distinction in their approaches. Edmundson's heroes are the romantic poets, whose ethic is given over to a rather grandiose, vainglorious, and heroically virile drama of transcendence, whereas the heroines of Brogan's novels are engaged in the routinely and traditionally discredited feminine work of forbearance, endurance, and cultural survival.

3
Abandoning Hope in American Fiction
Catalogs of Gothic Catastrophe

> Write in order not simply to destroy, in order not simply to conserve, in
> order not to transmit; write in the thrall of the impossible real, that share
> of disaster wherein every reality, safe and sound, sinks.
> —Maurice Blanchot, *The Writing of the Disaster*

Disaster Capitalism

"Disaster," as Eric Cazdyn reminds us in his introduction to a 2007 special
issue of *The South Atlantic Quarterly*, is contingent, "is that moment when
the sustainable configuration of relations fails, when the relation between
one thing and another breaks down" (647), as opposed to a crisis: "there is
something necessary about a crisis, something true to the larger systemic
form. Crises occur when things go right, not when they go wrong" (649). Increasingly, critics have consequently emphasized the paradoxically necessary
place of *disaster* rather than *crisis* within globalized systems of capitalist ac-
cumulation, most notoriously, perhaps, in Naomi Klein's 2007 bestseller, *The
Shock Doctrine: The Rise of Disaster Capitalism*. More importantly, as Cazdyn
insists, disaster obviates the utopian promise of revolution, which is predicated on the possibility of transforming accumulated crises into possibility:
Any new thinking of revolution today, then, must reckon unflinchingly with
the genuine predicaments of unredeemed disaster. "Compared to so much
wishful thinking," Cazdyn concludes provocatively, "bleakness and despair
are always a more productive starting place from which to forge new political and intellectual projects" (661).

Several critics have commented on the recurrent emergence of apocalyptic themes and images in the aftermath of the 9/11 attacks, the ubiquitous
"rhetoric of fear and apocalypse that pervades our contemporary politics
and culture" (175) as Marilyn Michaud puts it in her 2009 study of American gothic; but these fears, as she demonstrates, have "a long echo" (175).
Curiously enough, and for reasons that no doubt have much to do with a
rather horrified resistance to Reaganism (by which I refer to the entire ethical
and social apparatus mobilized during the "decade of greed"), selected gothic

works of American fiction from the 1980s and after provide such a starting point. This chapter will briefly consider four very different and very difficult works, each of which to a greater or lesser extent dispense with the available mechanisms of hope: I will address in particular Gerald Vizenor's *Darkness in Saint Louis Bearheart* (originally published in 1978; republished as *Bearheart: The Heirship Chronicles* in 1990); Patricia Highsmith's *Tales of Natural and Unnatural Catastrophes* (1987), Leslie Marmon Silko's encyclopedic *Almanac of the Dead* (1991), and, from a slightly later date, E. L. Doctorow's *City of God* (2000). The first three are works that Edmundson largely scants in *Nightmare on Main Street,* his survey of the terrain. For Edmundson, as I argued in the close of chapter 2, popular works of postmodern gothic aimed to achieve what he terms a "facile" transcendence; yet these three novels, despite divergent stylistic orientations and thematic concerns, invoke apocalypse and, with considerable relish, describe an imminent and unavoidable social collapse. The 1980s were marked by the most corrupt political administration in American history, during which, domestically, an attack on hard-won labor rights was accelerated and environmental regulations scrapped, when the gap between the wealthiest Americans and the economically dispossessed increased dramatically, and when, abroad, a sequence of military interventions (e.g., Lebanon, Nicaragua, Afghanistan) opened up an unfettered world market and so freed a hitherto regulated set of "deterritorialized" flows of migrant labor, populations, ideologies, networks, and capital— when, in short, a newly "globalized" capitalism emerged, particularly after the collapse of Soviet-style communism in the Eastern bloc, the ramifications of which we are only beginning to sift through and understand a quarter century on.[1] Even as I write, at a moment when the consequences of deregulation have become glaringly clear, the spectacular collapse of financial institutions on Wall Street threaten to destabilize the world economy. Whether this turns out to be a crisis that can be managed (and thus offer new possibilities for investment) or marks what some commentators have called the end of capitalism remains a very open question.

The popular culture of the time was ambivalent, at best, about these developments, and broadly characterized by what might be termed a "celebratory critique" of Reaganesque society; Bruce Springsteen's mega-hit, "Born in the USA" (1984), an energetic lament for the post-Vietnam bad faith shown to the industrial working classes, was, not so weirdly after all, cited by the then president as one of his favorite songs; similarly, such films as Sylvester Stallone's *First Blood* (1982) both mourned the betrayal of working classes and kept faith with an American mythic complex of unlicensed libertarianism and the old frontier promise of rebirth and social renewal through masculine violence, whereas *Wall Street* (1987), an ironic critique of junk-bonds culture and insider trading, was taken to be an etiquette guide for rapacious social climbers. For a variety of reasons (the Cold War, the shift in cultural production toward the fabrication of individual subjectivities) that I have documented more extensively elsewhere,[2] literary production had, by this time, largely withdrawn from the American social contract and was no longer complicit with the project of imagining America; there are no whole-heartedly Reaganite "novels," even if various works of the time—from Bret Easton Ellis's scandalous *American Psycho* (1991) to Bobbie Anne Mason's *In Country* (1986) to Tom Wolfe's *The Bonfire of the Vanities* (1988)—variously diagnosed the symptomatic malaise occasioned by the administration's abandonment of New Deal and Great Society policies of inclusion. Aesthetically, postmodernism, symptomatically endeavoring to spin free of the gravitational tug of historical causality, as Fredric Jameson has famously argued, generated the most critical buzz at the time. A mournful minimalism (e.g., Raymond Carver, Ann Beattie) was likewise in the ascendancy, which blurred across class lines at times into yuppie agonistics (Ellis, Douglas Coupland, Tama Janowitz); it was not until the 1990s, however, that critics began to notice another literary phenomenon of the time, which, in hindsight, appears the bleakest and thus, as Cazdyn intimates, the most compelling literature of radical dissent: postmodern gothic. In closing this study of haints, my working thesis is that contemporary gothic, anticipated in these and other novels, might be a form of cultural production specific to disaster capitalism.

In his post-9/11 writings, Jean Baudrillard concurs with Cazdyn's diagnosis, although he poses the more radical possibility that catastrophe beggars the imaginations of reformers and revolutionaries alike, suggesting that disaster, though an endemic function of power within contemporary capitalism, unleashes forces through what he terms a "logic of reversibility" that propel us into an absolute beyond: "What looms on the horizon with the advent of globalization is the constitution of an integral power, of an Integral Reality of power, and an equally integral and automatic disintegration and failure of that power" (23), he asserts in *The Intelligence of Evil*. Baudrillard reflects on "events that break the tedious sequence of current events as relayed by the media, but which are not, for all that, a reappearance of history or a Real irrupting in the heart of the Virtual (as has been said of 11 September). They do not constitute events *in* history, but *beyond* history; beyond its end; they constitute events that have put an end to history. They are the internal convulsions of history. And, as a result, they appear inspired by some power of evil, appear no longer the bearers of a constructive disorder, but of an absolute disorder" (126). Consequently, he concludes, "generalized exchange—

the exchange of flows, of networks, or universal communication—leads, beyond a critical threshold we passed long ago, to its own denial, which is no longer then a mere crisis of growth, but a catastrophe, a violent involution" (128). An initial question to pose, then, is what *marks* that critical threshold, and at what juncture have we, however unawares, crossed it?

For Baudrillard, at any rate, any attempt to salvage or reconstruct a humanist credo from the shambles of representation would now constitute a rearguard gesture, as would efforts to renegotiate any form of the social contract, however provisional. The supplementary question I wish to pose in what follows, thus, involves whether *representation* itself is up to the task of confronting the consequences of disaster, or gesturing beyond, however bleakly or pessimistically. What might the fictions of "absolute disorder" look like? Entertainment, to be sure, is designed to deflect our attention and to channel the panic of consumers, via a moral sleight of hand whereby virtue triumphs; this is the case, despite a recent spate of Hollywood films that are happy to substitute an existential black humor for moral certitude (think, for example, of the Coen brothers' 2007 *No Country for Old Men*). Films that dramatize the issues at stake with any sort of historical and political precision (2007's *Rendition,* for example) or imaginative perspicacity (as with the rather splendid *Children of Men,* in 2007), still tend to hold forth the promise that the ethical actions of individuals might make a small difference, and so provide a measure of consolation. The philosophy embedded in such narratives aims, in what might be termed a solipsistic utopian gesture, still to console.

Even so, the rhetoric of disaster weighs heavily and insistently upon the available (and dominant, in contemporary American cultural production) narrative logic of therapeutic redemption; prevailing stories of healing, closure, resolution, transcendence, love, comprehension, and so forth promise us a rather facile passage through and beyond traumas that turn out not to be so traumatizing—disasters that turn out not to be so disastrous—after all. In other words, we might speculate that contemporary cultural productions tend to project an awareness of "disaster" and then shy away from the implications, by dramatizing (usually in "personalized" terms) a safe passage through it; consider the crowd-pleaser *Fight Club* (1999), wherein the implications of the anticorporate mayhem are shrugged off as the narrator cures himself through a therapeutic act of self-directed violence and winds up getting the girl; the film defuses its potentially radical political and social message by constraining it within a story of personal therapy and redemption. Such a process involves what Edmundson, in his assessment of popular American gothic idioms, terms the commodified affect of "facile transcendence," or what Terry Eagleton, in an age more resolutely ideological, perhaps, than our own, had in mind when he argued that novels dished up "an ideological resolution of real contradictions" (176).

The work that concerns me, by contrast, imagines an apocalyptic endgame to looming social crises; rather than using the generic mechanisms of the psychological novel, these books fictively accelerate destructive social forces and tip them over into disaster, in an attempt to liberate the productive potential of despair. The most characteristically experimental or postmodern of these books, Gerald Vizenor's *Bearheart,* responding to the oil crisis of the early 1970s as well as to the flagging of the radical activism of the American Indian Movement (AIM), prophetically enough anticipates an America where the oil (which is to say, he remarks, the national "soul") has run out. Highsmith offers an ironic collection of various forms of apocalypse. Her writing, notoriously, is psychologically unsettling, as the safeguards of sanity in her characters guarantee no brakes against psychotic behavior; and, in her arch irony, she typically draws her readers into sympathetic complicity with all sorts of murderous machinations. Spurred by the 1978 media attention to the devastating effects of accumulated toxic waste in Love Canal and by the 1979 accident at Three Mile Island nuclear facility, and by the subsequent evasion of responsibility by the newly minted Reagan administration, the collected tales of catastrophe indulge political and economic perversions as well; in "Operation Balsam, or Touch-Me-Not," bureaucrats charged with overseeing public safety conspire to bury contaminated waste in leaky vessels underneath the football stadium of a large midwestern university; the culminating story, "President Buck Jones Rallies and Waves the Flag," highlights the irresponsibility of the Reagan administration's nuclear brinkmanship. In it, a presidential couple closely modeled on Nancy and Ronald Reagan spitefully causes a nuclear armageddon that destroys the entire planet. Silko's chiliastic *Almanac of the Dead,* perhaps the most staggering and difficult work of the period, is more sweeping in its scope, understanding contemporary environmental and political crises as symptomatic of the brutalities occasioned by the five-hundred-year occupation of the new world. In *Almanac,* the desert border city of Tucson, Arizona, "home to an assortment of speculators, confidence men, embezzlers, lawyers, judges, police and other criminals, as well as addicts and pushers, since the 1880s and the Apache Wars" (15) is situated at the "ghostly crossroads" of a struggle that involves the entire global population, living and dead. The armies of the dispossessed—indigenous peoples, slaves, drifters of every sort—enlist the forces of the spirit world to their cause and dream of a mighty apocalypse. Rather than offering an effort to redeem or reform capitalism, Silko's is a prophetic book that envisions and solicits the collapse of Christian and capitalist society, drawing on the anger of five hundred years. Finally, in a lengthier section, I will argue that Doctorow's novel points to and beyond the terrorism of September 11, 2001. Doctorow, to be sure, remains one of our most trenchant, if mournful, humanists, though I will argue that his work nonetheless dramatizes what he sees as a catastrophic alternative.

The Trickster's Laughter: Gerald Vizenor's *Bearheart*

Although these four works of quasi science fiction might be each characterized as dystopian, they have little else in common beyond a shared renunciation—or, in Doctorow's conception of "despairing hope" (93), a radical recalibration—of optimism.[3] Vizenor's *Bearheart: The Heirship Chronicles*, as Owens has commented, is persistently "upsetting" to readers, not merely because of its skewed ethics, unflinching bawdiness, nor simply as a consequence of its deep and often misogynist violence,[4] but also because it skewers conventional and sentimentalized representations of American Indians. In his own theoretical writing, Vizenor has emphasized the importance of a trickster and tribal literature working in the service of "postindian survivance," which will mean attacking and tearing down the "manifest manners," as he terms them in his collection of that subtitle,[5] that suffuse the ideologies of domination and that stricture and determine appropriate "ethnic" understandings: "Survivance is an active sense of presence, the continuance of native stories, not a mere reaction, or a survivable name. Native survivance stories are renunciations of dominance, tragedy, and victimry. Survivance means the right of succession or reversion of an estate, and in that sense, the state of native survivancy" (vii). As Owens argues, *Bearheart* is an attack on what Vizenor terms "terminal creeds": rigid or inflexible belief systems that we falsely believe allow us a measure of security in the universe. A satirical take on a standard spiritual quest or pilgrimage—the book references Chaucer, Spenser, Rabelais, and John Bunyan, among others—the novel depicts a motley group of pilgrims under the leadership of a protagonist named Fourth Proude Cedarfair, who are making their way transversely across the ravaged continent toward the Southwest. En route, in a series of comic allegorical episodes, they face a bevy of spiritual, ethical, social, philosophical, and sexual challenges and are compelled to confront problems of chance, necessity, and spiritual transformation. One by one, depending on the nature of their sins, failures of courage, or spiritual weaknesses, they are picked off: They drop out, are punished, or (most often) killed, in a paroxysm of poetic justice.

At one point, for example, the pilgrims encounter a horde of cripples who have been mutilated by cancers and deformed by chemical pollutions: "the blind, the deaf, disfigured giants, the fingerless, earless, noseless, breastless, and legless people stumbling, shuffling, and hobbling in families down the road" (145). One of the pilgrims, Little Big Mouse, who sentimentalizes these victims of petrochemical poisoning, begins to dance, in order to demonstrate her love for them; she is savagely raped and her body ripped apart:

> Proude stood back and roared in his bear voice from the mountains. He roared four times but the animal lust of the cripples had turned to evil fire. Sun Bear Sun climbed over dozens of crippled bodies. When he was near his little woman in the center of the pile he saw them pulling at her flesh with their teeth and deformed fingers. Others were taking frantic turns thrusting their angular penises into her face and crotch. Little Big Mouse was silent but the cripples moaned and drooled like starving mongrels. The lusting cripples slapped their fists, thrust their beaks, pushed their snouts and scratched the perfect flesh with their claws and fingers. The savage whitecripples pulled her flesh apart. Her hair was gone from her crotch and head and armpits. Her fingers were broken and removed. Her face was pulled into pieces, her breasts were twisted, her feet and legs pulled from her body. The cripples gnawed and pulled at her until nothing remained of Little Big Mouse. (151)

Grotesque as it is, this episode describes a literal demolition of sentimentality. The poor—the victimized, the dispossessed, the lumpen—will figure as the agents of revolution in many of these works, but it will no longer be enough to feel compassion nor even to speak on their behalf. Rather, as Jamie Skye Bianco asserts in reference to Silko, citing both Chela Sandoval's *Methodology of the Oppressed* and Hardt and Negri's *Empire*, "non European peoples of color represent a new transcultural and revolutionary social class, . . . 'the poor,' . . . [marking] a departure both from the Marxist politics of collective labor and those of post-industrial Euro-American working class" (9). I will return to the revolutionary potential of "the poor" as figured in Highsmith and Silko; with regard to Vizenor's indictment of sentimentalism here, however, it is enough to note that they are precisely beyond the available cultural mechanisms of representation itself.

To be sure, an optimistic reading of the book is available. As Owens argues, Proude, a "compassionate trickster" figure, a storyteller, and a shape-shifter, who is able to cheat death and who cultivates laughter and the principles of randomness, and his disciple, Inawa Biwide, arrive at Pueblo Bonito and "enter the fourth world as bears" (Afterword 253); his wife, Rosina, though herself viciously raped and left behind with her lover, the transgendered Sister Eternal Flame, are likewise "translated through the trickster's laughter into myth" and find "a new existence within the ever changing stories, the oral tradition. For all peoples, Vizenor, argues, but for the mixedblood in particular, adaptation and new self-imaginings are synonymous with psychic survival" (*Other Destinies* 240). Yet, what is key here, for the purposes of my argument, is the absolute indictment of the Anglo-American social contract.

The Spiritual Mob: Patricia Highsmith's "Red Slipper"

Highsmith likewise cedes narrative authority to a mob at various junctures in her story collection. Perhaps the most remarkable piece in *Tales of Natural and Unnatural Catastrophes* is the penultimate story, "Sixtus VI, Pope of the Red Slipper," in which a conservative Roman Catholic pope, modeled in some ways on John Paul II, stubs his toe during a trip to Latin America. The accident triggers a change of heart and he embraces liberation theology. When he is killed and martyred in an uprising, the people assume responsibility for their own social and spiritual power:

> A slow revolution was sweeping the world, but unfortunately causing a great number of deaths. In the next many approaches or attacks of the peasantry, even in the Philippines, the peasants and workers were more numerous than they had been in the skirmish in Bogotá that had killed the Pope, because they had time to assemble. The haciendas, factories, residential enclaves were prepared too with tear gas, firehoses, tall steel gates, and machineguns, but the fact was there were more peasants and workers than bullets. In many battles, the workers rushed over the bodies of their fallen, entered houses and took them over. Then began "confrontation," talking. The people were in the main calm, realizing their number and their power, and frequently cited the Church and God as being on their side. (159)

The tale in some sense leaves us hanging here; though Highsmith never pursues the consequences of these uprisings, she assures us, in closing, that it "was not a fad" and that the symbol of the pope, the "red slipper," remained "revolutionary," conveying to disciples of the cause that "I am a believer still" (161). In closing, Highsmith gestures toward an affirmative, revolutionary faith (the potential of which I will return to, in my discussion of Doctorow's premise of faith stripped bare of theological certitude).

The Uprising of the Poor: Leslie Marmon Silko's
Almanac of the Dead

That gestural affirmation bellows and resonates throughout Silko. Silko's *Almanac of the Dead* also describes a massive worldwide uprising of the indigenous poor, who advance on several fronts. Yet Silko's work moves beyond the satirical "survivance" of Vizenor and the cautionary, prophetic irony of Highsmith and resolves into a full-throated affirmation of catastrophe. She accomplishes this, in a more or less deadpan and declarative style, by moving beyond thresholds of representation: Rather than merely speaking *on behalf of* the dead and suffering, she enlists their voices; rather than merely speaking *on behalf of* the earth, as most environmental novels do, she articulates the emerging relations between the speech of the poor and the land itself, summoning into being what Baudrillard would term an "evil" that topples the novel toward an "absolute disorder." The novel speaks from the far side of disaster, from the far side, even, of death, and dismantles the no longer "sustainable configuration of relations" by positing a new language and a new community that might potentially emerge in that "beyond."

From dread emerges a new language and a new community. Leslie Marmon Silko, like Vizenor, a founding figure of the post-1968 renaissance in Native American writing, is a writer who rather gleefully appropriates gothic conventions as she sees fit; *Almanac of the Dead* gives us a heroine, Seese, on the run and a set of diabolically sadistic aristocrats. All of Silko's work, from her short stories and verse through to her more recent *Gardens in the Dunes* (1999), which is almost a parody of Ann Radcliffe or Wilkie Collins, comprises an inspired effort to enlist the sacred machinations of a demolished tribal past in a syncretic engagement with the potentials—and the devastations—of the contemporary. According to her scheme, history itself (under the sign of the European invasion of the Americas) has traumatically ruptured a mythic cosmology that would align legend, lore, ancestry, the land, the language, and community gossip in a seamless web with the most mundane of everyday events. "War had been declared the first day the Spaniards set foot on Native American soil, and the same war had been going on ever since: the war was for the continents called the Americas" (133). In Silko's ethical spiritualism, an endeavor that is syncretic rather than assimilationist, the armies of the dead want nothing more than the full repossession of the land: Indigenous peoples (and their miscegenated offspring—in the novel, Silko explicitly indicts racial purists) demand that Europeans go back to Europe.

Silko's chiliastic *Almanac,* consequently, invokes the whole of the Americas and Africa in a struggle in which even the dead are not safe. The motley armies of the dispossessed, of the poor, the vanquished, the dead, are on the move:

> The time had come when people were beginning to sense impending disaster and see signs all around them—great upheavals of the earth that cracked open mountains and crushed man-made walls. Great winds would flatten houses, and floods driven by great winds would drown thousands. All of man's computers and "high technology" could do nothing in the face of the earth's power.
>
> All at once people who were waiting and watching would realize the presence of all the spirits—the great mountains and river spirits, the great sky spirits, all the spirits of beloved ancestors, warriors, and old friends—the spirits would assemble and then the people of these continents would rise up. (425)

So Clinton, for example, a black veteran of the Vietnam war, now a drifter who helps to assemble an army of the homeless, describes his aspirations. Clinton has cobbled together a sort of vagrant's cosmology, composed of the miscegenated gods and goddesses of the Afro-Caribbean diaspora and Native Americans: "Clinton remembered the old grannies arguing among themselves to pass time. The older they got, the more they had talked about the past; and they had sung songs in languages Clinton didn't recognize, and when he had asked the grannies, they said they didn't understand the language either, because it was the spirits' language that only the dead or servants of the spirits could understand" (420). And Lecha, who has taken it upon herself to transcribe the apocryphal and fragmentary almanac of the dead, is a clairvoyant. She makes her living as a guest on daytime television talk shows, and assists the police in searching for the bodies of murder victims. Significantly, she can only converse with the dead: "They are all dead. The only ones you can locate are the dead. Murder victims and suicides. You can't locate the living. If you find them they will be dead. Those who have lost loved ones only come to you to confirm their sorrow" (138).

Finally, as Caren Irr has noted, the book rethinks and revitalizes the long-buried tradition of the American radical novel. Among the allies in this struggle that Silko describes is La Escapia, or Angelita, a renegade Marxist demagogue and double agent, who exhorts her people to the repossession of the land. For her, the Marxist understanding must be refigured as magical; the labor theory of value itself bespeaks an animist vision: "Marx understood what tribal people had always known—the maker of a thing pressed part of herself or himself into each object made" (520). "Poor Marx," she argues, anticipating Derrida's spectral rereading of *Capital,* "did not understand the powers of the stories belonged to the spirits of the dead" (521).

Baudrillard, to his credit, has noted the infectious link between aboriginal cultures and his own conception of evil.[6] In *The Transparency of Evil,* he writes:

> It is not even remotely a matter of rehabilitating the Aboriginals, or finding them a place in the chorus of human rights, for their revenge lies elsewhere. It lies in their power to destabilize western rule. It lies . . . in the way in which the whites have caught the virus of origins, of Indianness, of Aboriginality, of Patagonicity. We murdered all this, but now it infects our blood, into which it has been inexorably transfused and infiltrated. The revenge of the colonized is in no sense the reappropriation by Indians or Aboriginals of their lands, privileges or autonomy. . . . Rather, that revenge may be seen in the way in which whites have mysteriously been made aware of the disarray in their own culture. . . . This reversal is a worldwide phenomenon. It is now becoming clear that everything we once thought dead and buried, everything we thought left behind forever by the ineluctable march of universal progress is not dead at all, but on the contrary likely to return—not as some archaic or nostalgic vestige (all our indefatigable museumification notwithstanding), but with a vehemence and virulence that are modern in every sense—and to reach the very heart of our ultra-sophisticated but ultra-vulnerable systems, which it will easily convulse from within without mounting a frontal attack. Such is the destiny of radical otherness. (137–138)

In Silko's hands, the "vehemence and virulence" become postapocalyptic, even, we might say, postpolitical. Given the intolerable conditions under which so many live, illiteracy, poverty, rampant deculturation, workaday violence and terror, the task of any political literature, then, is to participate in the ongoing invention of the unborn people under new conditions of struggle. Silko, for example, thinks of her storytelling as a conjuring, a verbal sorcery to set or keep in motion the imaginary contours of a revolutionary desire that will not content itself with limited demands for sovereignty. In *Almanac of the Dead,* she envisions a massive upsurge of the dispossessed, living and dead, who begin to walk north across the continents to reclaim the land. Silko admits in the confessional of her prose to an avowedly naïve desire that Europeans (*Anglos,* to use the favored ethnic slur of the American Indian reservations) simply pack up and go back home, leave the New World, a desire, however intemperate, purist, utopian, or impractical, however explicit or muted, which we should acknowledge to be braided and laced through all pan-Indian politics and/or cultural enactments of resistance (from Tecumseh's uprising through Wovoka's ghost dance to the AIM and the Zapatista rebellion in Chiapas). Even so, her writing privileges the mixed-blood, her approach is relentlessly syncretic, a tactic, as Owens has pointed out, that takes non-Indian materials (the novel itself, the English language) and puts them to Indian uses; an assimilationist strategy, on the other hand, would swallow up and incorporate indigenous cultural patterns into a generalized or homogenized utterance. As one of her characters, a drug smuggler, proclaims in *Almanac of the Dead,* "we have no respect for borders." Calabazas teaches: "we don't believe in boundaries. Borders. Nothing like that. We are here thousands of years before the first whites. We are here before maps or quit claims. We know where we belong on this earth. We have always moved freely. North-south. East-west. We pay no attention to what isn't real. Imaginary lines. Imaginary minutes and hours. Written law. We recognize none of that. And we carry a great many things back and forth. We don't see any border" (216).

Silko's heroines and heroes, her valorized and disingenuous tricksters, her storytellers and shamans, are, as in so much Native writing, outlaws, when reckoned from a proprietorial point of view: adulterers, poachers, confidence-tricksters, cokeheads, revolutionary brigands, cattle-rustlers. They have no respect for borders. It is exactly this refusal of borders, coupled with an adamant, ubiquitous demand for (the return of the) land that we are compelled to gloss. This demand for land, this trajectory across the land, these movements, this upsurge, these armies of the dead: All the throngings that strafe, possess, and mobilize a voice, a language, the articulate mutation of location into locution, of locale into the vocal.

The world Silko describes is populated by those who have lived *in* catastrophe at least since 1492. In closing, I want to suggest how languages beyond catastrophe might—and must—emerge, in Silko and in other writers. We are confronted with the now irrefutably "globalized" dimensions of capitalist expansion, where activists, their backs to the wall at least since September 11, are compelled to articulate linkages between, say, the massacre of peasants in Colombia or Bolivia at the behest of Bechtel, the murderous dismemberment of tribal societies in Nigeria at the behest of Shell Oil, the Palestinian struggle for national sovereignty and the exponentially escalating Israeli "retaliation," the war in Afghanistan, and so on, to highlight only a few of the more newsworthy barbarisms of the New World Order. Throughout this chapter, I have endeavored to link contemporary gothic with market circumstances: In the aftermath and recognition of capitalist injustice, Marxism is, as Silko intimates, made magical, and revolution is imagined as something apart from workers seizing control of the means of production. Rather, it involves a gothic spawning of new life, out of the rotting corpse of everything dead and buried.

Deleuze has described a minor writing, which seizes upon such circumstances. What is sometimes missed by commentators on his conception, however, is the necessary link between global capitalism and the minor: that minor writing is something more than simply the writing of minorities; rather, it summons into becoming the potential of the poor. "One can't think," wrote Deleuze, "except in relation to the higher level of the single world market, and the lower levels of the minorities, becomings, peoples" (152). Minor writing, according to Deleuze and Guattari's conception, deploys a practice of collective enunciation and communal expression that summons forth a people, inaugurates a becoming. Such writing is not simply a way of setting oneself up as a representative spokesperson for a preexistent community, a people already there who might need, as in the Marxist experiment, their consciousness awakened to revolutionary fervor. Rather, a minority "is itself a *becoming or a process,* in constant variation. . . . Minorities have the potential of promoting compositions (connections, convergences, divergences) that do not pass by the way of the capitalist economy any more than they do the state formation" (D. Smith xliii). While oppressed minorities obviously and necessarily struggle for, among other things, rights, land, language, political recognition, autonomy, their struggles deploy passions and desires that elude standardized political models. Dispossession demands more—the struggle is for life, not merely concessions; in turn, catastrophe gothic envisions the living productions and productivity of bleakness, of despair, far beyond anything we might recognize as hope.

Faith-Based Initiatives: E. L. Doctorow's *City of God*

Doctorow concludes his theological and quasi-gothic 2000 novel, *City of God,* with an apocalyptic vision of New York as postmodern Babylon.[7] In the light of the subsequent attacks on the World Trade Center, the scenario appears almost brutally prophetic: "Prophets arise in their clerical robes to speak of evil, to speak of irreverence and blasphemy. They announce that the wrath of God has come down on the city of unnatural pride, the earthly city. They call upon the pious to destroy the city. And the unremarked God, the sometime-thing God, is alive once again, resurrected in all His fury" (271). Yet the full vengeance of a wrathful God is perpetually deferred. Dooms-day never arrives within the fictional confines of Doctorow's novel; not only is God absent, but so too are His prophets. The twist is that this apocalyptic vision is nothing but a "screenplay," a script-in-progress envisioned by *City of God*'s primary narrator, a writer named Everett. God's active interference (however mediated) in human affairs is nothing but a story, only a movie. To-day, divine justice is wholly a fiction.

It was never anything but, even in more entrenched ages of faith than our own. For Everett, a relentless "secularist," like Doctorow himself, world re-ligions were never more than spectacularly good (that is, effective or pro-ductive) stories. To Everett's mind, the social apparatus of Old Testament Ju-daism, for example, mobilized popular cultural mythologies that performed the social work of distinguishing between the sacred and the profane (or at least the mundane). The priestly caste in turn legitimated itself by mo-nopolizing upon the interpretation of the links and disjunctions between this world and the divine; under such a monotheist regime of signs, social order among the chosen people might thus be maintained by fetishizing the twin pillars of ancient Judaism: the book and the law. The two are the same, of course: In the name of one God, narrative transmutes itself everywhere into doctrine. Exegesis, for example, was essentially a critical enterprise that magically held forth the promise of a divine theodicy in the absence of any semblance of justice that might be observed in the normally dismal course of human events. In *City of God*, Everett muses upon the dilemma at a study group he attends at a synagogue of "Evolutionary Judaism":

> The biblical texts from the beginning were seen as enigmatic, as why would they not be, having been written in a language without vow-els or punctuation. And since they were supposed to be divine in their source, and therefore of a supernatural perfection, the scholars, priests and sages of antiquity felt called upon to explain the contradictions, un-God-like sentiments, unsavory passages, and less than noble acts of noble personages of the stories as well as whatever else could not be countenanced in its righteousness . . . by interpreting them metaphori-cally, symbolically, or allegorically, or by changing their meaning by adding punctuation, or opportunistically applying syntactical empha-ses, or by otherwise reimagining whatever they felt needed improve-ment if it was to be truly theologically correct. I was happy that eve-ning to recognize the venerable ancestry of hermeneutics. (114–115)

Yet, for Everett, hermeneutics—a collage of interpretive strictures, at best—no longer suffice. If stories, subject to multiple interpretations by virtue of their very unruliness, had always eluded priestly strategies of containment, then today even the discipline of rigorous interpretation has slipped its leash. The collapse and hyperacceleration of traditional ways of life, coupled with the endemic sufferings of the sad century just ended, make it an increasingly arduous task for the authorities of church or state (let alone the forlorn individual) to fabricate anything like coherent spiritual solace. Put simply, in a heterogeneous world of endemic distress, there can be no homogeneity of interpretation, no common law. Secular law is itself nonbinding, for a theist.[8] When the law of the land contradicts a "higher law," one is morally obliged to break the former.

Hence the interpretive and narrative difficulties of Doctorow's own cinematic collage. As Geoffrey Galt Harpham has noted, the ambivalence of "narrative itself and its relation to power, imagination, and belief" (29) are the central concerns of Doctorow's writing, and in *City of God,* Doctorow meditates on the precarious possibility of a fully *secular* ideal of justice. Insofar as we are uprooted from the bedrock of a common culture and adrift in the improvisational and free-floating narrative nexus of the information age, to what higher principals can human justice appeal?[9] In *City of God,* Doctorow deploys an almost stereotypical strategy of postmodern pastiche, which conspires to form an old theological lament: My God, my god, why have you abandoned me? Within the novel itself, stories, like the screenplays, fragments, erotic fantasies, dramatic monologues, and other frenetic jottings in Everett's notebooks, proliferate more or less wildly and at random; they do not submit to a common system of interpretive arbitration. The philosopher Jean-François Lyotard, who has famously described the postmodern condition as characterized by the collapse of theojuridical "meta-narratives," describes such a state of affairs in *The Differend:* With the breakdown of meta-narratives, in which isolated and unique stories might once have discovered their rationale in a common story of teleological redemption, how can competing schemes establish a common ground? In *Just Gaming,* Lyotard and Jean-Loup Thébaud aptly appropriate the term *paganism* to describe "a situation in which one judges without criteria" (16). Even though they everywhere provide a plentitude of ethical examples and delimit the contours of our identities, the stories that circulate freely in the contemporary cultural spheres (of which New York City is itself both symbol and symptom) can no longer be counted on to *teach* us authoritatively; nor do they fully *explain* us to ourselves. Events themselves not only surpass and beggar interpretive strategies, they elude the patterns of narrative containment itself. The predicament of history throws us outside of both meaning and shape, the twin guarantees of a universe governed by order. And so, as Everett reckons, our stories are simply *too sad to be true:* "We must conclude that given the events of the twentieth century of European civilization, the traditional religious concept of God cannot any longer be seriously maintained" (53).

Doctorow's cautionary tale, then, consists of a twofold warning. To begin with, he isolates the ethical menace of basing any kind of moral principles (that is, a meaning to be acted upon) on any set of scriptures. Stories are stories are stories: If they touch us, they nevertheless cannot be taken as guides to behavior, except in the loosest and most provisional sense. As Doctorow has written in a brief but key statement of the ethical principles of literature, "Texts That Are Sacred, Texts That Are Not," sacred texts carry an injunction to truth that secular literary texts, at least those that are worth their salt, renounce:

> The scriptures of Judaism, Christianity, and Islam were produced or revealed in those ages when stories were all people had—and when their invention was the word of God. Those residual communal texts that have made us who we are were hard-won instructions for survival and discoveries of the intellect that were configured illustratively, sometimes in verse, so as to be transmittable by memory from person to person, long before they came to be written. They gave counsel. They connected the present with the past. They bound the visible to the invisible. They distributed the suffering so that it could be borne. Like the stories of today, they made no distinction between fact and fiction, between ordinary communication and heightened language. . . . Language was enchanted. And the very act of telling a story carried a presumption of truth. . . . God, in his authorial perfection, is not to be questioned. (53–54)

By contrast, then, "literature does not call upon followers. . . . It purveys moral complexity, paradox, irony, pathos, human failure, and the failure, comic or tragic, of human institutions. It is the mirror of the irresolute human soul" (52). Yet, one can ask, apart from poignant testimony to felt experience, can narrative containers even dissimulate a rational "understanding" of the human predicament? Consequently, in *City of God,* Doctorow likewise interrogates the very relevance of storytelling (divinely inspired or otherwise) to contemporary events. In this novel, it seems, narratives are themselves inadequate to the brutal complexity and misery of human life.

Religion, always gothic, has gone apocalyptic. Doctorow's task, therefore, is to critically interrogate the destiny of faith itself in such a world, amid such collapses. If God is to be found at all, Everett is told, He cannot be found in the desert, in the holy lands, in the scriptures, in ascetic contemplations or rigors of any sort. If God exists, He—and any faith we might have in Him—must be differentially, ruinously, manifest: "It's here in the Metro-Diaspora. Whatever it is, it's in this bloody, rat-ridden, sewered and tunneled stone and glass religioplex" (214). New York is, for better or worse, the titular city of God, where religions persist, and in many ways are more popular than ever; but they are precisely that: "pop" religions. That is, religions are no longer deeply embedded in the social structures of everyday life, but circulate as unregulated spiritual consumer goods in the free-for-all of the postmodern marketplace of salvation. Christianity, Buddhism, Islam, and Judaism are less ways of life than lifestyles. Because faith is farcical, it is all the more dangerous.

Which is, after all, why we go to the movies. In Doctorow's depiction of the contemporary world, Hollywood has largely shouldered the burden of justifying God's ways to man and (on occasion) to woman, and religions are simply glossy serial advertisements for an epic costume drama, with the Rapture as its happy ending: "Choose Christ!" Movies, in Doctorow's book, deliver the fantasy of a justice (and an apocalypse) that theology can no longer fully supply, a cultural condition to which such films as *The Passion of the Christ* (2004) by Mel Gibson and Kevin Smith's *Dogma* (1999), in different tempers, both attest. In other words, films (and popular culture at large) have usurped the social functions of religion. They make sense of a senseless world, offer a dramatized interpretation of our transfiguration and provisional salvation. On screen, if nowhere else, good triumphs, evil is punished, and the hero is resurrected. The world is thus made new, and we, the viewing public, are absolved of all our imperfections. Every blockbuster unveils a miniteleology. It is as if film itself has become a god:

I swear to you, something is going on with movies *in a way even the people who make them don't understand.* I mean, something weird has happened, so that I am convinced that the people who ostensibly make them are no more than instruments of the movies themselves, servers, factotums, and the whole process, from pitching an idea for one, and getting the financing and finding a star, I mean, the whole operation, while seeming to depend on the participation of directors, producers, distributors, and so on, and for all the animosities and struggles among them . . . all of it is illusion, as the movie is supposed to be, a scripted reality, whereas it's the movies themselves that are in control, preordaining and self-generating, like a specie with its own DNA. (*City of God* 108–109)

Hollywood, not God, is the hidden power at work in the unfolding of historical events. And Hollywood is fully incarnate. If the "death of God" was already a modernist cliché, a death certified (in Europe, at least) by the horrors of trench warfare, the lagers, the gulags, and so forth, then what we might call the *postmodern* crisis of faith centers around His ubiquitous resurrections. And still, even as millenarians are perpetually mistaken in their predictions of the last days, so too does the promised final judgment degenerate into a predictable sequence of increasingly shopworn "grand finales." There is always a sequel. Commodity fetishism is no doubt a perpetually elusive form of faith. Advertising appeals to our yearning for transfiguration, but perpetually defers the promise of corporeal rebirth. The Christ we purchase at the Mall of In God We Trust, Inc., cannot make us whole any more than our new brand of deodorant, or a new sports utility vehicle. We are promised peace and given credit counseling.

But the celluloid god, if he is always with us, also fails. The proffered peace is illusory, transitory, and ephemeral. For, Doctorow asserts, we continue to grieve, to mourn, and to suffer, and nothing religion or Hollywood can offer comes near to approaching a genuine commentary upon—or consolation for—the barbarous conditions of mundane existence. Redemption is itself farcical. And so God is challenged in the novel, in a set speech that echoes all of Job's humility and piety, while rejecting his religious masochism:

The world You have created, or that has used You to create itself, suffers not only the headline killers of our century, the contemptuous rulers of tribes and nations, but the miserable, wretched numbers of the rest of us, who inhabit the back pages and work in symbolic emulation of their spirit, living fervently to enrich ourselves at the expense of others, so that even in our most advanced industrial democracies life is adversarial, and the social contract breaks down continually, as if we were not meant to be justly governed nations but confederacies of murderous gluttons. . . .

Do You not find this a grave challenge to your existence, Lord, that we do these things to one another? That for all our theological excuse-making, and despite the moral struggles and intellectual and technical advances of human history, we live enraged—quietly or explosively, but always greedily enraged? Do You not find it an unforgivable lapse of Yours that after thousands of years we can no more explain ourselves than we can explain You? (267)

The tragic theme at the center of Doctorow's oeuvre throughout the 1980s and '90s has been the perpetual eclipse of the American left, the repeated failures and disenchantments of progressive politics. He is, as Fredric Jameson pointed out (to Jameson's own dismay and consternation), "the epic poet of the disappearance of the American radical past" (*Postmodernism* 21), and that history itself, uncoupled from class struggle, has as little political weight as a movie. The political, social, and cultural failures that Doctorow's work recounts and fictionalizes, however, are mourned in the full recognition of the ongoing necessity of political revitalization, however utopian or paradoxical this might seem at first glance. In contradistinction to Jameson's more or less fatalistic view of Doctorow, Michelle M. Tokarczyk has accentuated his "skeptical commitment," his "continual revision of American myth" (20). The precise historical and theological problem at the heart of his turn of the millennium novel might be best characterized as *the necessity of hope in the absence of faith*. The answers supplied by the available religions, argues *City of God*'s alternative protagonist, the Reverend Dr. Thomas Pemberton, are either specious or vicious, and too often both: "How, given the mournful history of this nonsense, can we presume to exalt our religious vision over the ordinary pursuits of our rational mind?" (66). And if, as Francisco Collado Rodriguez argues in one of the very few critical commentaries on *City of God*, Doctorow insists on a wild and unflagging "longing for metaphysics" in the contemporary world, nothing in the novel suggests that we can consent that this moves us "beyond the relativist impasse" (Rodriguez 59).[10] Rather, the book compels us to meditate on the productive possibilities of a hope tempered by despair and longing within a world where differences are in violent collision and transcendent judgments are impossible.

The characters in *City of God* suffer from what once might have been called despair; once, spiritual torpor; and today, good sense. For, as antitheists, agnostics, and a few honest scribes and priests have pointed out, murder is too often rationalized by divine sanction. In Doctorow's novel, the Rabbi Sarah Blumenthal explains: "In the twentieth century about to end, the great civilizer on earth seems to have been doubt. Doubt, the constantly debated and flexible inner condition of theological uncertainty, the wish to believe in balance with rueful or nervous or grieving skepticism, seems to have held people in thrall to ethical behavior, while the true believers, of whatever stamp, religious or religious-statist, have done the murdering. The impulse to excom-

municate, to satanize, to eradicate, to ethnically cleanse, is a religious impulse. In the practice and politics of religion, God has always been a license
to kill" (255).

So He is, once again, and once more Doctorow proves uncannily prophetic. God promises an apocalyptic "truth" that history, Hollywood, and the
human condition all refuse to provide, and it is a truth that, inevitably, must
be violently enacted. For what good is faith without bad works? Osama bin
Laden's henchmen, for instance, target the degenerate "relativism" of American hegemony and Western decadence. The perfectly cinematic attacks on
the World Trade Center and the Pentagon were irrefutably real, and their success, for true believers, is nothing more than a concrete demonstration that
God has acted against America. The act of violence, political or religious, is
always tempting, as Walter Benjamin has argued, for it dramatically enacts
its own burden of proof. Humanity, writes Benjamin, "is impelled by anger to
the most visible outburst of violence that is not related by a means to a pre-
conceived end. It is not a means but a manifestation" ("Critique" 294).[11] Thus
the perceptible "irrationalism" of Islamicist terrorism, which is why so many
commentators are tempted to speak of the phenomena in terms of pure evil:
Unlike acts of terrorism that demands a homeland for Palestinians, for example, or an end to the British occupation of Ireland, al Qaeda's September
11 attacks had (let's be frank) no immediate political point to make.[12] Terrorism is the ultimate performative utterance, for it instantiates that which
it claims to be true, with the entire world as witness. Terrorism makes a new
truth, God's truth or Allah's, come into being. It is—and proves—the hand of
God at work in the affairs of humans. Doctorow laments in "The Politics of
God": "How, given the increasingly warlike pietism around the world since
the end of the Cold War, can we avoid concluding that fundamentalism is
the truest expression of religious sensibility? . . . The religious modality may
now be declaring itself tenable only in its simple atavistic readings of the ancient texts" (89–90). The violent destruction of life and property, occasioned
by nothing less than a longing for metaphysics, an act of love gone wrong,
as Michael Hardt has theorized, puts an end to all doubt, all skepticism, all
relativism, all debate: "I refute it thus!" Noting that terrorists respond to the
self-same ecumenical agonies and frustrations as the rest of us, and offering
his own ironic, skeptical humanism as a provisional antidote to doctrinaire
religiosity, Doctorow continues to speculate on the possibilities: "Is it possible that the terrorism of the most devout and self-martyring Muslim has,
at its heart, that same provisional and so even more despairing hope? Apart
from the rare experience of ecstatic revelation, the religious commitment is
a matter of education—some would say indoctrination—or family loyalty, or

conversion inspired by political bitterness. Does the leap of faith ever land? It does for the prophet, the revelator" ("The Politics of God" 93). On September 11, 2001, as in Doctorow's novel, the wrath of God has come down on New York/Babylon, the city of unnatural pride, the earthly city. And, although Hollywood had anticipated and envisaged the attacks in a thousand and one movies from *Die Hard* to *Independence Day* to Tim Burton's satirical *Mars Attacks!*, this was no movie.

So, without Bruce Willis to save us, Osama bin Laden's point *must* be acknowledged. One cannot say, with Baudrillard, that the attacks on the Pentagon and the World Trade Center did not take place.[13] Yet anyone doubting the currency of "postmodernist" simulacra would have done well to plant herself before CNN broadcasts on the morning of September 11th. Not only were the videotaped attacks on the World Trade Center compulsively described as resembling special-effect scenes from a Hollywood disaster film, but, in the worrying absence of any legitimate spokesperson, CNN was forced to turn to Tom Clancy, a writer of popular thrillers, for "expert" commentary. Indeed, in an ironic version of life intimidating art, Hollywood was compelled to edit or block the release of a handful of upcoming thrillers, whose scenes of mass destruction were thought to replicate too closely, too harrowingly, the terrorist attacks.[14] Like the twin towers of concrete and steel, the most enduring, trenchant, and dominant of American institutions, an entire ideological-corporate apparatus of "spin," was teetering on the brink of collapse.

For the events of September 11 were not your run-of-the-mill suicide bombings (with all due respect to all who have been killed or wounded in smaller-scale acts of terrorism). In only a few minutes, a handful of zealots had been able to strike with unthinkable success at the very heart of American economic and military power: They took out the Pentagon with a boxcutter. In those early hours after the attacks, it seemed as if America had been devastated not only by these atrocities, but, in their aftermath, by the pointed absence of a language in which to wrestle a coherent sense of—and from— what had happened. We suffered not just a staggering loss of life, property, and status, but from an ideological rupture of potentially devastating (but also potentially liberating) consequence.

It may help to reconsider some of the context. The bombing of the Alfred P. Murrah building in Oklahoma City had itself already cut close enough to the ideological bone, for the full horror of that episode had been Timothy McVeigh's successful dissimulation of an "average American." McVeigh, who with David Koresh is one of the unacknowledged martyrs and guiding spirits of today's tea-partiers, and whose philosophical orientation was squarely in the mainstream of Great Plains racist antifederalism, could in no way be demonized as an "outsider." McVeigh was too tantalizingly "one of us" to be readily dismissed as a nut. As René Girard has argued, sacrificial scapegoat mechanisms function to preserve the symbolically immaculate nature of social communities. When a threat is isolated, a criminal condemned, a cancerous cell-growth excised, the body politic is magically healed and made whole again. Communities solidify themselves in the face of an external threat; but when the agent of chaos is recognized as internal (the enemy within), sacrificial and theatrical acts of catharsis become necessary. The white mob lynches sexually aggressive black males, for example, to preserve the homogenous integrity of white womanhood, and thus protect the fantasized social body from "miscegenation." It does not matter that miscegenation is always already a historical given in the American South, nor does the "guilt" of the perpetrator make any real difference, as, according to the sacrificial logic of the scapegoat, any black male is a potential rapist. As Girard insists, the victim is arbitrarily selected for punishment, and the magical function of such rituals is to disavow one's own guilt. If "he" is the sinner, "I" must be the elect; if "the other" is the brutalized black body, "I" must be the wholesome and inviolate white. So Girard describes the birth of a nation:

> The universal spread of "doubles," the complete effacement of differences, heightening antagonisms but also making them interchangeable, is the prerequisite for the establishment of violent unanimity. For in order to be reborn, disorder must first triumph; for myths to achieve their complete integration, they must first suffer total disintegration.
>
> Where only shortly before a thousand individual conflicts had raged unchecked between a thousand enemy brothers, there now reappears a true community, united in its hatred for one alone of its number. All the rancors scattered at random among the divergent individuals, all the differing antagonisms, now converge on an isolated and unique figure, the *surrogate victim*. (79, original emphasis)

Given McVeigh's own fair-haired, blue-eyed demeanor, the border between a fantasized "them" and a consolidated "us" (America) seemed increasingly permeable, and so the hoariest of scapegoating mechanisms, public lynching, was dragged out in fine American fashion. McVeigh, the guilty party, was executed by the federal government, and we were reassured, once again, that the enemy within was safely "without." I remember watching on the local Oklahoma City news broadcast a vigil held at the Murrah memorial on the morning of McVeigh's execution. One teary-eyed witness told how, at the minute of his death, she saw the sun break over the horizon. It was a "new dawn" for America. His benevolence certified by the clarity of daybreak—clearly, a sign from above—God was on our side, once again.

In contradistinction to faired-haired, blue-eyed boys, Arabs are easily enough demonized, on racial and religious grounds, and Osama bin Laden himself initially provided a convenient scapegoat for national demonologists. When bin Laden proved curiously elusive, Saddam Hussein, whom something like 70 percent of Americans were convinced was the culprit who masterminded the 9/11 attacks, was there to take the fall. As Girard insists, the victim is arbitrarily chosen; his guilt is entirely irrelevant. Yet, al-Qaeda, terrorism itself, is at once easier and more difficult to contain within the scapegoating logic Girard describes. Easier, because a marked difference (e.g., of religion, of language, of culture, of skin color, of dress) distances Mid-Easterners conveniently enough from stereotypical Americans, and a consequent xenophobic and racist fear of foreigners can be easily mobilized. Threats by native Aryan supremacist groups have never inspired the Department of Homeland Security to change the color-coded alert levels. And if the Tea Party and fellow travelers, who have successfully criminalized "looking Latino" and banned ethnic studies in Arizona, prove to have as much political as they have social traction, we will need to confront the consequences of a grass-roots, postmodern, genuine American fascism.

For while the personification of menace can be relegated to those who are visibly different, the real danger is that the threat is ubiquitous. Suiting up for a global struggle with no end in sight, "homeland" security wants it both ways: The home must be understood to be a safe haven, and any threats to it must be considered foreign, threats from the outside. And yet, the foreign might be found anywhere, even at home, even in one's neighbor, even in one's own self. Terrorism comes from out of a clear blue sky, attacking the unsuspecting and unvigilant; it (rather brilliantly) uses the technologies of the first world against itself. Terrorism is contagious, unpredictable, cancerous, and far more pernicious in its capacity for dissimulation than communism had been, even in the heyday of the Cold War. There is no evidence whatsoever that terrorists are "taking orders from Moscow," so to speak (despite the efforts to portray bin Laden as the evil genius behind all attacks on American interests). The enemy is felt, quite palpably, to be nowhere and everywhere, and potentially anywhere. We may want to bomb the bastards back to the Stone Age, but who are they? Where are they?

It is not that the logic and mechanisms of scapegoating are no longer operative (quite the contrary). But they are no longer fully functional, no longer capable of pretending to guarantee a full justice. As Girard argues, the magical practice of generating community is a relentlessly sacred affair:

The production of community through violent retribution is the very demonstration of divine power (and so it is no accident, nor simply a polite sop
to religious conservatives, that the Bush administration declared the war on
terror to be a "holy" war and a "crusade"). But it seems that such rhetoric,
such rituals, are no longer "fooling" anyone. Scapegoating reveals itself as—
merely—scapegoating. The revelations, for example, that Saddam Hussein
was merely a tin-pot dictator and not the diabolical genius that the military
needed him to be indicates as much. Bin Laden himself may well be guilty,
but his guilt or innocence is not the issue. It remains to be seen whether
Americans can fantasize ourselves as whole again now that he has been killed.
Or, at the very least, our sense of security will be mighty short-lived.

As the September 11 attacks dramatized, the confidence with which truth
and justice are being served is noticeably inflated. The compulsively repeated
assurance that America was America again seems almost panicky, hysterical.
So establishment powers scramble to cobble together a discourse of reassurance. The point—one I have been stressing in various ways throughout this
study—is that our national mythologies, such as they are, are inadequate to
comprehend or digest the full enormity of the assault. The government was
itself inoperative for several hours, and we waited until the early afternoon
to hear from anyone in national office, let alone our leader, who was being
hop-scotched across the country in Air Force One. Bush's "tough talk" in the
weeks following seemed impostured, defensive, even petulant at the time,
and seems even more so today as the bunglings of his administration become
clearer and clearer. The fantasy of American power unveils itself as fantasy.
The edifice "America" as a divinely ordained national fiction staggers.

All subsequent events can be read as a more or less frantic effort to recoup
upon a loss that can in no way be made good. Droning chants of "USA!"
at the World Series to the contrary, the putative and doubtful "success" of
the wars in Afghanistan or Iraq notwithstanding, it will be some time before "America" is again "secure." As critics point out, and as Bush himself acknowledged (at least in the speeches immediately subsequent to the attacks),
the deposition of a criminal regime in Afghanistan, even the recent execution of bin Laden, however celebrated, has not fully reassured the national-
ists who demand proof. A holy crusade to rid the world of evil (and Bush had,
initially, promised nothing less), is a different kind of holy war, fully apocalyptic. Subsequent administrations will have, to be sure, to reckon with the
global responsibilities that Bush has high-handedly evaded, at least insofar
as military and political success will, in the long run, rest upon transnational
coalitions. Obama's foreign policy, which so far has stressed a cautious real-
politik, even in the seemingly endless, largely disastrous, war in Afghanistan,

seems to bear this out. But the political upshot—and this is perhaps the greatest long-term danger—may turn out to be hyperisolationist; the war itself, in an Orwellian turn, may serve to justify the legal institutionalization of a regime of paranoia.

For his part, Doctorow warns against the emergence of a full-fledged, good old-fashioned, fascism: "It becomes a political commonplace resisted not even by theorists of the democratic left that totalitarian management, enforced sterilization procedures, parentage grants issued to the genetically approved, and an ethos of rational triage are the only hope for the future of civilization" (272). We will have to hope desperately that this vision is, well, only a movie. Even so, when the surrender of civil rights to a fantasized "freedom" from terrorism is mentioned in a serious political discussion, there is adequate reason to be alarmed.

And America's forced reengagement with religious thinking has troubling overtones. Another consequence of the attacks, we were told in the days following, was that Americans had begun to "pray" again: Churches, mosques, temples, and synagogues were filled to capacity, spontaneous prayers and mourning would break out in public spaces, and even agnostics flocked to orchestrated assemblies and sing-alongs. Although it is doubtful that Americans had ever stopped praying (it is apparently among the most "religious" countries on earth, with a remarkably high percentage of people who claim to believe in some sort of divine principle), religious leaders hoped to inspire a great awakening. The populist Jerry Falwell launched a jeremiad against the unholy conspiracy of witches, feminists, lesbians, and liberals, who had spurred God's judgment on an unregenerate nation. President Bush himself invoked the deity, describing the upcoming war as one between good and evil (thus, by extension, it is perfectly understandable that, judging by the temper of the blogosphere, liberals are today considered tantamount to Satanists).

So, what is to be done? Doctorow's counter to the grandiosities of fanatical Islam and/or radical Americanism is itself relatively modest: an inquiry, both passionate and skeptical, yet again, into the premises and possibilities of fabulation. "At this point," he tells us in a closing moment that turns the book's narrative back in upon itself, "we are introduced to the hero and heroine of the movie, a vitally religious couple who run a small progressive synagogue on the Upper West Side" (272). The protagonist is the former pastor of Saint Timothy's, the Reverend Dr. Thomas Pemberton, a divorced, depressive Episcopal priest undergoing a progressive crisis of faith. Pemberton loses first the brass cross from his church, Saint Timothy's, which is stolen and mysteriously reappears on the roof of an uptown synagogue. Pem, as he is called, is subsequently stripped of his parish when St. Tim's is desanctified, along with his vocation and his faith. Everett, Pem's interlocutor throughout, initially wants to cover the story of the disappearing cross. Their discussions over the course of the novel function as a sort of catechism of Pem's disillusionment, and Everett becomes increasingly obsessed with tracing out the trajectory of a decent man, for whom neither religious nor political faith will suffice (despite a temperamental commitment to both).

Pem's theological inquiry is simple enough, on the surface: What good is faith without good works? In other words, Pem figures, it praises God more to go about His business than it does to fetishize His existence. Pem, whose temper is almost compulsively scholastic, is also troubled by the failure of religions to appeal to the intellect. The traditional reply, that faith begins where reason is forced to retreat, seems to him patently thin and evasive. The clichéd definition of faith as a conviction that transcends rational understandings, he argues, is an offense to God, who after all created our intellects as well: "The sensation of God in us is a total sensation, given to the whole being, revelatory, inspired. That is the usual answer to the questioning intellect, which by itself cannot realize sacred truth. But is the intellect not subsumed? Does the whole being not include the intellect? Why wouldn't the glory of God shine through to the human mind?" (65).

Finally, Pem is insulted by the insipid moralizing that attends the interpretation of sacred texts. "Nothing shakier in a church than its doctrine," he muses (42). Again, it is the conflation of narrative into universal principles that is most dubious: "Migod, there's no one more dangerous than the storyteller. No, I'll amend that, than the storyteller's editor. Augustine, who edits Genesis 2–4 into original sin. What a nifty little act of deconstruction—passing it on to the children, like HIV. As the doctrine of universal damnation, the Fall becomes an instrument of social control. God appoints his agents plenipotentiaries to dispense salvation or withhold it. I don't know about you, dear colleagues, but history has a way of turning a harsh light on my faith" (67). The "story," given Pem's necessary suspension of belief, degenerates into a multitude of stories. His is a *Pilgrim's Progress* in reverse, wherein he is compelled to stray farther and farther from the path of righteousness. Doctorow's narrative is itself fragmented, episodic, aphoristic, even chaotic. It reads in large part like a writer's notebook, full of unfinished and hurriedly scribbled observations, fantasies, and works in progress, mostly screenplays. In one proposed screenplay, for example, an ex-CIA operative is able to exact personal retribution on a Nazi war criminal, living inoffensively in an American suburb. He is aided by providence; but such things only happen in the movies. The book is punctuated as well by the meditations of some of the greatest minds of the twentieth century: Einstein, Wittgenstein, and Frank

Sinatra. Each is looking to do it "My Way," to evade what the character Wittgenstein terms "God-drenched thinking" (190). Wittgenstein's own philosophical project involved cleansing philosophy of all its metaphysical and moralizing nonsense, in an effort to reduce philosophy to the purity of statement, which referred to nothing beyond itself. Yet Wittgenstein himself was forced to confront the essential impurity of statements. If statements are not divinely guaranteed, if they cannot be understood to refer outside of themselves (though they always do), then they can only exist in a context of endless language games. There can be no common measure.

Lyotard, consequently, describes the various operations of power under such conditions of paganism. There is, Lyotard asserts, a multiplicity of justices: "Justice here does not consist merely in the observance of the rules; as in all games, it consists in working at the limits of what the rules permit, in order to invent new moves, perhaps new rules and therefore new games" (100). Lyotard's only caveat to this is that there is, he claims, "the justice of the multiplicity, whose universal prescription is the prohibition of terror"—that is, "the blackmail of death towards one's partners" (100).

Nothing is true, and all is permissible, except terror. Thou shall not kill. Doctorow subscribes to such a prohibition, assuredly, and even endorses it. But there is nothing to guarantee its universal applicability, sadly. All evidence points the other way, in fact. People seem to murder as happily in the absence of God as in His presence, and if it is not today the atheists who are doing the killing, it is only because circumstances conspire against it: They have certainly done their share. The only remaining ethical task, today—and it may well be a kind of sacred duty—is to shirk doctrinal imperatives, to free up such language games, to put them once more into play, rather than to arrest them in the stranglehold of genre. For the writer Everett, the ultimate and perhaps only appeal of religion itself is in its scripture, its narrative and metaphorical possibilities: "Beyond that, as a writer, I am only fascinated by the power of this hodgepodge of chronicles, verses, songs, relationships, laws of the universe, sins, and days of reckonings . . . this scissors and paste job that is in its original form so terse, inconsistent, defiant of common sense, and cryptically inattentive to the ordinary demands of narrative as to be attributed to a divine author" (114–115).

Pem, for his part, is voluntarily condemned to ferret out one of the more insidious language games to have been perpetrated. He turns to the central crime of the previous century, the Holocaust, and listens to the voice of the man, a survivor, who is to become his father-in-law. The voice documents Nazi atrocities in the ghetto in what is today called Vilnius, and tells of the smuggling out of a transcribed record of many of the deeds done. The papers were smuggled from the ghetto, and hidden in a church, later to be confiscated by the Red Army. Pem, God's "detective" as he ironically calls himself, travels to Lithuania and subsequently to Russia and retrieves the document from the vaults of the KGB. He hands it over to American authorities, in the slim hope that it may help to bring a Nazi fugitive to justice.

But perhaps such things only happen in movies. At any rate, his has been an act. The question Doctorow leaves us with, then, is this: What good are good works without faith? They may, in fact, be of no use at all, and they certainly have nothing to do with redemption. "For all of its powers," insists Doctorow, "literature does not call upon followers" ("Texts" 52). Good—the best of—works may involve nothing more (and nothing less) than telling different stories.

Conclusion

American Innocence

I opened by suggesting that 1944 was the last year America might reasonably claim its innocence; in a brave new world of technological menace, amid the paranoid fantasizing of the Cold War (note how science fiction during the fifties and sixties transforms itself from a progressive to a paranoid discourse; Harlan Ellison replaces H. G. Wells as a symptomatic writer), one might expect the impostures of innocence to be cast into the dustbin of history. And yet, the ongoing project of America seems to have depended on the imagination of innocence at every juncture. The wellsprings of a fabulated American "innocence" seem inexhaustible. Consider, for example, the rhetoric of innocence and trauma that followed the terrorist attacks of September 11, 2001. Innocence, which is always constructed in retrospect (innocence only manifests itself once it is lost, or threatened), is the very denial of haunting; or rather, it involves a heroic evasion of the fact that one's actions are implicitly entwined with the destiny of others, in the face of all evidence to the contrary. Such innocence, then, is always in some sense threatened, haunted. As a construct by which we adjudicate and parcel out responsibility, the category of innocence needs to be threatened, or haunted: It would not otherwise exist or be understood *as* innocence. This is why crimes are assumed to be more heinous when they target "innocent victims" or involve hurt to "innocent" bystanders. Innocence unknowingly (or half-knowingly) solicits, seduces haunting, as in Henry James's deeply perverse novella, *The Turn of the Screw,* wherein the ghoulish pederasts, Peter Quint and his lover, Miss Jessel, are seductively summoned from their watery graves by the allure of the children, Miles and Flora. Indeed the pedophile cannot *help* him or herself (to acknowledge how the will of pedophilia is crippled is not at all to blame the victim). And pedophilia in whatever form (the murder of innocents, the murder of innocence) may be the central phenomena of gothic; it is no accident, as

Edmundson notes, that a rather hysterical discourse of satanic pedophilia emerged in Reagan's America of the 1980s, a society that sorely needed to refabricate its own innocence. The production of a retrospectively defensive innocence (an innocence always, alas, lost), which disavows responsibility (rather than being the simple opposite of "guilt"), is at the heart of American mythography. Alexis de Tocqueville puts it this way: "Not only does democracy make every man forget his ancestors, but it hides his descendents and separates his contemporaries from him; it throws him back forever upon himself alone and threatens in the end to confine him entirely within the solitude of his own heart" (99), going on to speculate about the inevitable appearance of mysticism and "religious insanity in such a country."

As Gordon elaborates, for Nathaniel Hawthorne, America is likewise a land without ghosts. In the preface to *The Marble Faun*, Hawthorne insists that we inhabit "a country where there is no shadow, no antiquity, no mystery, no picturesque and gloomy wrong" (15). Or, as Morrison says, "We live in a land where the past is always erased and America is the innocent future in which immigrants can come and start over, where the slate is clean. The past is absent or it's romanticised" ("Living Memory" 10). Consequently, the "great tradition" in American letters, our eminently usable past, embellished as much in Greenwich Village as in Hollywood, "has taken as its concern the architecture of a *new white man*" (Morrison, *Playing in the Dark* 15), and was until recently thought to be a decidedly masculine imperative to exorcise one's ghosts; its conventional theme, as the critic Mickey Pearlman argues, is the fear of historical entrapment, which assumes the form of a peculiar, and peculiarly American and heroic, exceptionalism: "the chronicle of the solitary hero, of man alone, man against society, man as individual, endlessly testing his strength and durability against his own resources on a mythic adventurous journey to epiphany and knowledge" (1). The dramatic and sacrificial logic of this tradition demands that society itself and the social conflicts that compose it be reduced to a mere backdrop, an arena or stage for individual heroism. The triumphal Yankee tradition involves a necessary reduction of social constraints—class, geographic origin, parentage, race—in accordance with the American myth of the "self-made man," crystallized as early as Benjamin Franklin's *Autobiography* and resurrected, almost facetiously, in the campaign rhetoric of Al Gore and George W. Bush, who both struggled to disavow the influence of their own founding fathers. In America, according to such an assimilationist logic, we are compelled to give up the ghost. And yet ghosts continue to insist on our duties to the past. In Anne Sexton's remarkable story "The Ghost," a Victorian spinster, of Puritan lineage, refuses even after death to abandon a fierce and violent love for her namesake niece: "Indeed, perhaps, an American ghost does something quite different, because the people of the present are very mobile" (226).

Yet insofar as American literature itself has taken upon itself the task of articulating the dimensions of this new, very mobile creature, the American, it has been gothic from the get-go. Long assumed to be the inaugural text of serious American fiction, Charles Brockden Brown's 1798 *Wieland; or, The Transformation: An American Tale,* an immigrant story, of sorts, explicitly acknowledges the founding act of cultural dispossession at the root of the production of the American. Torn between a temperamental cowardice and an unshakeable religious zealotry, and finding England intolerable, old Wieland makes for the New World. "He had imbibed an opinion that it was his duty to disseminate the truths of the gospel to the unbelieving nations" (16), Brown tells us ironically, and "the North American Indians naturally presented themselves as the first object for this species of benevolence" (17). He is, predictably enough, unsuccessful; the Indians simply laugh at Wieland until he abandons the cause. Shortly after, however, his mysterious death ensues. Even though Brown is careful to provide rational explanations for many of the purportedly supernatural events of the novel, it is the "inexplicable" flash of light that sets the gothic mechanisms of the convoluted tale in motion. Brown is obviously and deliberately modeling his fiction upon gothic best sellers in Europe. Nonetheless, "in a land without castles or ghosts" (as the blurb for the Anchor Library edition of *Wieland* points out), the social tensions that various historians have seen as underwriting gothic anxieties must be reimagined.

The survival of what has been repressed within a consolidated myth of progress is not simply a matter to be taken up by students of genre, I think, although even a cursory glance at the national literary canon, a canon traditionalized over the course of this century and today, perhaps, in the process of being dismantled, would remind us of the surprisingly neglected centrality of American gothic: Charles Brockden Brown, Washington Irving, Edgar Allan Poe, Nathaniel Hawthorne, Mark Twain, Herman Melville, Emily Dickinson, Ambrose Bierce, Pauline Hopkins, Henry James, Edith Wharton, Gertrude Stein, Robert Frost, William Faulkner, Djuna Barnes, Flannery O'Connor, William Goyen, Thomas Pynchon, Rudolfo Anaya, Joyce Carol Oates, Toni Morrison, William Kennedy, Cormac McCarthy; the list goes on.[1] Nor am I merely pressing you to an awareness that, as the historian Simon Schama points out, the historical novel, even more so than the romance, "problematizes the reality of the present" ("History and the Literary Imagination").

For our history has always been, in Tillie Olsen's phrase, "dark with silences" (23) and there is another more subdued and ghastly America that we should reckon with, and another, and still another. The limits of a constituted "national" identity mark the struggle for dominion over the past, an ongoing competition over the shape and destiny of a set of histories that cannot be considered simply collective. This is a matter of revenants. Ghosts throng at these occult borders, at the wounds of memory, where history shudders, where even the historicization of cultural images partakes of a disenchantment, clamoring for an unveiling of what has been occluded or hidden over. What Pierre Nora has termed *lieux de mémoire,* sites of memory, are complex, or "knotted," with phantoms, as Gordon would have it. Gordon accentuates the "tangled exchange of noisy silences and seething absences" (200), whereby we are condemned to live among ghosts, who make their presence known variously, through orature—speaking in the voice of others—and possession. Animation, ritual, performance, carnival are all enactments of the spectral embodiment of need. The war over, and involving the dead, which Walter Benjamin speaks of in his theses on history, is not completed; we stand at the "crossroads where ghostly signals flash from the traffic, and inconceivable analogies and connections between the events are the order of the day" ("Surrealism" 183).

For ghosts are everywhere in contemporary American fiction, and this book has only skimmed the surface of what could rightly demand a much longer study. They show up in the work of writers who would seem to share nothing else in common. I am thinking of the haunts and magic in Erdrich's *Tracks,* and Silko's *Gardens in the Dunes,* as well of Maxine Hong Kingston's *The Woman Warrior,* for example, in which the narrator comes to voice her own stories amid a world of ancestral and modern ghosts. The ghosts of Francis Phelan's past are central to William Kennedy's meditations on masculinity in his best seller, *Ironweed,* and Norman Mailer writes *Harlot's Ghost,* a secret personal history of the CIA. *Ghosts* is the middle part of Paul Auster's *New York Trilogy,* a playful epic thriller of isolation, estrangement, loneliness, and exhaustion. Ghosts array themselves in August Wilson's *Fences,* in Gloria Naylor's *Mama Day,* in Paule Marshall's *Praisesong for the Widow.* In this context, too, we should consider the frontier gothic of Cormac McCarthy's border trilogy, not to mention his own postapocalyptic novel, *The Road.* In Toni Morrison's work, most significantly, the dead always refuse to stay buried or silenced, as in the remarkable novel of Reconstruction, *Beloved,* as we have seen. Time and again Ana Castillo employs figures of ghosts to flavor her bitterly satirical magical realism. In Alison Lurie's elegant collection of stories, *Women and Ghosts,* phantoms haunt domestic spaces and everyday preoccupations become sinister, foreboding, and force the women in them to confront the demons of their own femininity. *Madeleine's Ghost,* a highly conservative, Catholic, and grossly sentimental novel by Robert Girardi conjures the ghosts of old New Orleans.[2] And the Canadian writer Michael Ondaatje has weighed in with his story of the civil wars in Sri Lanka, *Anil's Ghost.* Or consider Doctorow's own 1994 *The Waterworks,* which is, among other things, an extended homage to Wilkie Collins (it evens ends with a double wedding!). The book is set in New York, in the depression year, 1872, and begins when a young layabout and part-time journalist catches a glimpses of his dead father riding a white omnibus through the city streets. McIlvaine, the narrator, mistakenly insists: "this is not a ghost tale":

> To me, a ghost is [a] tired and worn-out . . . fancy. . . . I abhor all such banalities. I am extending myself in a narrative here. . . . I would not so hazard myself on behalf of some hoary convention, heaven help us all. This is not a ghost tale. In fact I'm wrong to even use the word *tale.* . . .
>
> But if you're entrenched in the Parlor Faith, let me remind you that by your own dicta, ghosts don't come in crowds. They are by nature solitary. Second, they inhabit defined spaces, such as attics, or dungeons, or trees. They are sited to do their haunting—they are not detached and collected and given rides about the city in public stages.
>
> No, the world I am spreading out for you here in the flat light of reality is the newsprint world, with common, ordinary, everyday steamboat sinkings, prizefights, race results, train wrecks, and meetings of the moral reform societies going on simultaneously with this secret story invisibly on the same lines. (96–97)

It is the coexistence of these two worlds that makes the ghost story—the consubstantiation of the real and impossible—possible. Similarly, T. Coraghessan Boyle's *World's End* tells the story of Walter Truman van Brunt, whose very literal "collision with history" is occasioned by hauntings, visions, and visitations. In this troubling 1987 book, set in 1968, which shares some of Doctorow's obsession with the sad history of American radicalism, the ghosts of a lost tribe of Hudson Valley Indians will return to claim their rights to the land that had been cheated from them by Dutch tradesmen and poltroons some three centuries earlier. Incidentally, this novel is about the betrayal of the radical tradition in the year 1968; the hero, haunted by ghosts, refuses to learn from them and ultimately betrays his friends—his haunted birthright condemns him to replay the historical patterns that have clamped down on alternative possibilities.

For the excluded, identity has too often been a matter of historical destiny or even doom; since 1968, and even before, different marginalized communities have involved themselves vocally in the distinctly American process of achieving an identity through self-invention, self-production, and self-articulation. Yet it is precisely this tension, this ghostly hinge between past and present, between historical destiny and the fabrication of one's own destiny that demands a renegotiation, a continuous rebargaining. The "self" is never whole or autonomous, never self-sufficient; it is generated from a past that is never fully knowable, from a historical unconscious wherein dwells both the repressed of our history—the violence too painful to speak—and the alternative, routes never taken, all of which still continue to haunt and possess us, that claim us. As Morrison says, "although history should not become a straitjacket, which overwhelms and binds, neither should it become forgotten. One must critique it, test it, confront it and understand it in order to achieve a freedom that is more than license" ("Interview" 114). And, in a finely ironic but impassioned appeal to cultural critics, E. San Juan, Jr., insists that we need to get "beyond the platitudes of identity politics" as well as "beyond celebrating fluid identities, hybridity, borderline or liminal bodies, uncanny deconstructive ventriliquisms setting 'post-colonial' gurus as new breed." Rather, "we need to wrestle with the task of historicising the cultural symbols that construct identities and ontologies of self-representation" (82).

Many contemporary American writers, particularly (but by no means exclusively) women and ethnic writers, are, to resurrect a phrase, looking backward, and attempting to invent alternate pasts. They are often concerned, as Morrison is, with the ongoing clarification of *who we are* in society rather than with elaborating the myth of fleeing social constraints on the one hand, or, on the other, affixing their imprimatur on the status quo. The interrogation of who we are demands, I argue, the continual investigation of who we have and who we *might* have been, and by implication, who we might yet still become. The project of inventing a past can function in terms of what the poet Adrienne Rich had in mind when she spoke of "writing as re-vision," an attempt to resee the past again, and to excavate its buried possibilities, to liberate the voices, the sufferings that have been covered over by time and tradition. Women's writing, for Rich, will not become an escape from the confines of a specific historical or social situation, but rather will involve the painful effort of finding a dwelling in a history of one's own—a history that has been banished, silenced, and used against one. In so doing, the writer might liberate her own capacity for self-articulation. It strikes me, to conclude briefly, that American fiction is still in the business (and make no mistake, it is a business, whatever sensibilities we wish to cultivate), of generating alternatives, of considering, with all the generosity of which literature, still, remains capable, of what Doctorow's narrator terms the "surplus of a bustling democracy" (99).

Emphasizing the improvisational, adaptive, and syncretic nature of modern ethnicities, Werner Sollors cautions against reductive understandings of modernization and commercialization as forces merely of assimilation or homogenization: "ethnicity is continuously created anew and . . . assimilation and modernization take place in ethnic and even ethnocentric forms" (245). In his appreciative survey of ethnic autobiography and fiction of the 1970s and '80s, Michael M. J. Fischer underlines a few very important considerations. Ethnicity is hybrid, he writes: "Ethnicity is a process of inter-reference between two or more cultural traditions. . . . Ethnic memory is . . . thus future, not past, oriented" (201). For contemporary writers, at least, investigations of a communal past, the "postmodern arts of memory," are routes through which new forms of consciousness, identity, and subjectivity may be wrought: "the search or struggle for a sense of ethnic identity is a (re-)invention and discovery of a vision, both ethical and future oriented. Whereas the search for coherence is grounded in connection to the past, the meaning abstracted from that past . . . is an ethic workable for the future" (190).

Ethnicity, future-looking, if encoded in arcane symbols and old narratives, emerges from a specific, if complicated, sense of exclusion, and so Fischer points out that "transference, the return of the repressed in new forms, and repetitions are all mechanisms through which ethnicity is generated" (207). It should come as no surprise that women writers in particular have seized upon these conditions, as nondominant communities often tend to be, so to speak, culturally matrilineal. Thus "this sense of the continuity between the natural and supernatural is often nurtured by cultural traditions other than a white Eurocentric one. So, American women writers with roots in minority cultures seem even more likely to accept the supernatural. In African-American and Native-American cultures, family ghosts, like living family members, are simply part of experience. They can be healing and supportive, and can bring information crucial to survival" (Carpenter and Kolmar 12–13). I would add that the ghosts of our national family can be threatening, dangerous, greedy, and divisive as well, as in Morrison or the novels of Erdrich, where haints are "very fierce and instructive" as O'Connor says of ghosts (45). Since the 1960s, women writers, and ethnic women writers in particular, look to the supernatural, as Bonnie Winsbro has effectively argued, in order to articulate "an effective self-definition" in relationship to the community, tribe, and family. Thus Winsbro emphasizes the "role of the individual's belief in supernatural forces in his or her individualization" (6). Permitted or destined a countertradition to draw from, to quarrel with, the contemporary and continued (re-)invention of gendered, ethnicized selves tries to steer a path between the Scylla of competitive individualism, and the Charybdis of historical entrapment.

Ghosts participate in this dialectic, between the production of identity as self-invention (a uniquely and supremely American ideal), and identity as historical destiny, or even doom. It has been the prerogative of various "marginalized" communities to interrogate and seize a forcibly silenced history in order to put it to play as one of the most significant elements in their own ethnicized self-fashioning. One claims one's heritage, so to speak, even where it has been brutalized.

At issue in the twenty-first century will be the cultural implications of the vexed dialectic between past and present, between dead and living, between national identity and ethnic diversity at various historical moments, whenever a fantasized "America" has been staked out. We are compelled to conjure the ghosts that haunt self-sufficiency (the Emersonian ethic) as if it were a sacrificial act. What will it mean for Americans today to invoke Doctorow's "surplus of a bustling democracy" (99), the ghosts of the slaughtered, the silenced, the forgotten? By "ghosts," I mean that which survives, singular, jealous, persistent, and beckoning—specters, absences that refuse to absent themselves, which would rise from the graves to which a national history has hastily consigned them. For me, this is the manner of muckraking appropriate to a haunted contemporary American cultural theory. Those writers that continue to interest me, for example, are those who are mediums, invoking the dead and the silenced, obsessed with the potential and alternative histories of the violently excluded. Morrison, who considers herself to be writing "for the village, for the tribe. Peasant literature for *my* people" ("An Interview" 253), insists that tribal dimensions overflow the borders of life and presence. She writes in turn "[f]or all these people; these unburied, or at least unceremoniously buried" (Morrison and Naylor 585).

What we are on track of here are the immense difficulties constructing a "national" heritage in so varied a country, and we are compelled to emphasize the pointed and vexing failure of "memory" to reconcile post–Civil War United States. The plethora of Civil War novels, films, television serials, books, and memorabilia, of all kinds, of historical reenactments of major battles, all suggest the urgency of our sorting among competing historical claims. Although contemporary fiction has served my argument admirably, it is not simply a question of privileging the contemporary novel, for the project should cover forgotten or neglected writers as well, not to mention popular cultural practices, and the work of critics and commentators who take up, so to speak, the abortive project of national "reconstruction." Much attention should be devoted to those ghosts who inhabit the no-man's land between the various accounts given of this historical epoch, Reconstruction: the renditions, in turn tragic and shabby, offered by W. E. B. Du Bois in 1903, with *The Souls of Black Folk,* and again in 1935, in *Black Reconstruction in America,* who invokes the "swarthy spectre" haunting national historiography. Reconstruction is perhaps the nation-building enterprise built large; a project that was, in Du Bois's eyes, less a failure than an effort that was abandoned. Significantly, Du Bois, a master of various different rhetorical idioms (the polemical, the rational, the sentimental), opts for a gothic idiom when describing racial dispossession, which results in African American "double-consciousness," described as otherworldly, uncanny:

> After the Egyptian and the Indian, the Greek and the Roman, the Teuton and Mongolian, the Negro is sort of a seventh son of seventh son, born with a veil, and gifted with second-sight in this American world,— a world which yields him no true self-consciousness, but only lets him see himself through the revelation of the other world. It is a peculiar sensation, this double-consciousness, this sense of always looking at one's self through the eyes of others, of measuring one's soul by the tape of a world that looks on in amused contempt and pity. One ever feels his two-ness,—an American, a Negro; two souls, two thoughts, two unreconciled strivings; two warring idols in one dark body, whose dogged strength alone keeps it from being torn asunder.
>
> The history of the American Negro is the history of this strife,— this longing to attain self-conscious manhood, to merge his double self into a better and truer self. In this merging he wishes neither of the older selves to be lost. He would not Africanize America, for America has too much to teach the world and Africa. He would not bleach his Negro soul in a flood of white Americanism, for he knows that Negro blood has a message for the world. He simply wishes to make it possible for a man to be both a Negro and an American, without being cursed and spit upon by his fellows, without having the doors of Opportunity closed roughly in his face. (364–65)

So too the recuperative dramatization by D. W. Griffith in his 1915 *The Birth of a Nation.* It is, decidedly, no accident that on the eve of an overseas war Griffith codifies the definitive, comprehensive formal language of a narrative cinema that will be put to the century long service of spectacular salesmanship.[3] Griffith's cinematic achievement is the expressive medium in which the message—the teleological triumph of white purity—will be best served up. Griffith instructs us in a highly controlled, if naturalized, "reading" strategy designed to regulate the semantic unruliness of cinema, to locate and constrain cultural threats through narrative containment: the simplification and allegorization of social conflicts, the indulgence of spectacle and mock suspense. He aims as early as 1915 to situate cinema at the heart of national culture and aspires pedagogically to produce discriminating—though not critical—viewers. As Ralph Ellison points out, with the emergence of a national cinema and cinematic technique, a more or less institutionalized dehumanization of blacks in political life "became financially and dramatically possible" (*Shadow and Act* 266). And Ellison's verdict, which accentuates the gothic dimension of fantasmatic nation-birthing, is exactly to the point: "If the film became the main manipulator of the American dream, for Negroes that dream contained a strong dose of such stuff as nightmares are made of" (266).

This is not to suggest that the film, as it is received and contested across the country, is ideologically closed; Du Bois's NAACP organized protests at the time, and the film continues to disconcert historians of cinema. Griffith very self-consciously inaugurates the century-long legal and social wrangling over censorship.[4] Neither is it coincidental that the professional historian and warrior for democracy, Woodrow Wilson, testifies to the "truth" of Griffith's film. It is less a matter of the historical amnesia than of the mediated choreographies and lived enactments of an agonistic social mnemonics. Consider the propaganda films of the "new" South from the 1970s and '80s—*Fried Green Tomatoes* and Martin Scorsese's *Cape Fear*[5] are good examples—which strategically split Southern history into distinct regions: one wherein racial bigotry and masculine violence are redeemable (Alabama in *Fried Green Tomatoes*), and one wherein they are excessive and must be purged (Georgia). Alternatively, the televised trial of O. J. Simpson, on the one hand, a public figure who embodies (and refigures for a consumer economy) the sexual anxieties that catalyzed the lynch mob, tapped into a surreptitious and semiconscious dread of what we might call, contra Norman Mailer, the "Negro white," who nonetheless continues to incorporate a sexual threat to Anglo-Saxon integrity. So too the semipublic trial of Timothy McVeigh, on the other hand, who acted on the distrust of federal intervention that is a specific heritage of the post–Civil War South.

The tensions of this heritage have been exacerbated over the past few decades with the deindustrialization of the northern cities and the resettlement of technocrats among the suburban sprawl of the so-called Sun Belt.

Remember that the Branch Davidian massacre, which seems to have spurred on McVeigh, was initially prompted by David Koresh's possession of illegal firearms, hardly considered a "crime" in Texas. Both of these highly fraught public events, which can serve to bracket and highlight the internal, domestic vexations of the global policeman that America has aspired to be in the New World Order, should be evidence enough of the persistence of the struggle over the meaning, heritage, and direction of historical "reconstruction" in popular understanding (Staiger 139–153). Morrison, who considers Bill Clinton, the former Southerner in the White House, in some sense "black," is the coeditor of a 1997 book of essays on the Simpson trial, pointedly entitled *The Birth of a Nation'hood.* For Morrison, the ghost here is Simpson as "dead man golfing" (and whatever sympathy or horror he evokes occludes and represses the actual corpses in the case, those of Nicole Brown Simpson and Ron Goldman). The Simpson trial is a perversely gothic fantasy predicated on the unmentionable assumption of white supremacy, which echoes the overt supremacism of Griffith's film: "The film *Birth of a Nation,* based on the novel *The Klansman,* gathered up and solidified post–Civil War America's assumptions of and desires for white supremacy. The Simpson spectacle has become an enunciation of post–Civil Rights discourse on black deviance. Both of these sagas have race at their nexus" (xxvii).

Birth: the language of reproduction is hardly coincidental to this discussion, for bloodlines are at issue here, along with the suppression of women's active presence in the formulation of national identities. Griffith's film defends the Klan, who must preserve the integrity of white womanhood against the threat of black rape (that, historically, it was white men who commonly raped black women is precisely the point: In the mythic birth of the nation, blood must be purified through the suppression of the African American woman's participation). Thus the cult of white womanhood depends on the fantasy of an ideal of purity and integrity in nationalist epic: The nation is symbolically born by protecting her from the threat of foreign infection. Gothic logic, in turn, traditionally requires establishing and maintaining a distinction between the ideal woman as the pure vessel of truth and the woman who, understood as threat, must be turned progressively or instantaneously, into a corpse—and publicly displayed as such. Such is the case even with Morrison; Sethe's mother in *Beloved* can be remembered only as the mutilated, violated, assassinated body.[6] In whatever form, difference must be suppressed, and as embodied in woman, must be murdered. And yet, in what I am terming *abortive epic,* this ghost of difference is precisely that which returns to haunt any cultural formation that struggles to keep the past at bay.

The imagined community of nation is produced by segregating the difference within identity, by banishing woman, by segregating ourselves from both living difference and the dead past. The melting pot is mediated by the potboiler: As with the magazine novels of Pauline Hopkins, for example, the ghost has been in melodrama a more or less traditional device for exposing miscegenation, the dirty little secret at the heart of the American melting pot, which the racialist thinking dominant throughout the nineteenth century conspired to overlook. The uniquely American apartheid established as the law of the land by the *Plessy v. Ferguson* decision (1896), uprooted the "one blood" heritage of Spanish and French New Orleans and replaced it with the legal fantasy of "separate but equal" institutions, thereby occluding class and ethnic complexity in favor of an assimilable white America contrasted to black. As Joseph Roach documents, the decision participated in inventing and establishing racial categories that echoed the segregation of the dead, the combined efforts of metropolitan theory and colonial practice. Octavio Paz, in his essay "Mexico and the United States" included in *Labyrinth of Solitude* distinguishes between North and Latin America by suggesting that, as opposed to a logic of hierarchy and integration in Spanish rule, we in the North have been handed over to a mythic logic of democracy and exclusion. So too Spillers, thinking of Faulkner's "bastard" Jim Bond, demonstrates that the construction of an imagined America involves, paradoxically, the negative work of "minority communities": "it is the ascribed task of such communities to keep the story of difference under wraps through the enactments and re-enactments of difference in the flesh. The single basis for the myth of national unity is raised, therefore, on negation and denial" (9). This is true even in the South, where "national" identity has no doubt been most bloodily contested.

Americans—mobile, acquisitive, competitive, individualistic—are traditionally charged with historical amnesia, and our popular culture is targeted for the ways in which it ruthlessly commodifies history, experience, sensibility, knowledge, and even our critical facilities. In the United States, "the relationship between history and memory is peculiarly and perhaps uniquely fractured" (Frisch 6). Our individual and collective pasts have been violently severed from our present via a range of techniques that substitute simulacrum for experience and community. History may not—yet—have proven itself to be over, despite the putative global triumph of market capitalism in 1989, but historicity, as Jameson likes to remind us, is on the wane.

It is a cliché, however, an oversimplification, to argue that the media and the market combine to traduce traditional historical sensibilities. If the postmodern condition can be characterized as pathological, it is a historical pathology. Nora writes that "we have seen . . . the end too of ideologies that prepared a smooth passage from the past to the future. . . . Indeed, we have seen the tremendous dilation of our very mode of historical perception, which, with the help of the media, has substituted for a memory entwined in the intimacy of a collective heritage the ephemeral film of current events" (284–285). As Michael Kammen comments, Americans have fashioned for ourselves "an entrepreneurial mode of selective memory" (535). Whenever we strike a deal with history, even if we choose to relegate it to the radically Other, we pay a price. The testy, fragile, doomed peace that we hash out with history, individually and as a nation, is haunted by the possibility of a truly radical pluralism, which only glimmers as ghost, ghost of past, and ghost of potential.

If today, then, the problems of flight and solitude, the possibilities of "lighting out for the territories," are no longer the concern for younger writers in America, particularly women writers, particularly black and ethnic women writers, and if a concern with disparate identities and one's fitful location in history and the social field are increasingly the subjects of contemporary fiction, then I think we can say, safely, if provisionally, that the problem fiction persists in dramatizing is the problem of living in difference. How can we live in difference? The challenge, as I've written elsewhere, is whether we can imagine a world of difference that is not already a world of strife (*Raids* 248). The question, for me, is whether culture can accommodate not only our hopes but also the hopes of the dead. The past is a nightmare that I am trying to indulge here, and the imagining of a future will involve surrendering to these ghosts, with all the delicious and incantatory rigor of a sacrificial ritual.

Were I so incautious as to venture that American culture, indigenous as well as global, popular as well as elite, mainstream as well as marginal, has a heart, I would say that at its heart is a fantasy of self-empowerment, a willed deliverance from the strictures and dogmas of an authoritarian past. Identity politics, for example, begins with so-called minorities seizing the power of self-naming. The self in my formulation is a rather evasive entity, as I argued in chapter 1, and the inability—the undesirability—of our ever assigning limits to the self is a continuous theme, for the self is always and everywhere haunted by that which is—by those who are—Other. At issue here too is the bugbear of American constitutional politics, the inescapable tension between individual liberties and group emancipation. I recognize that this is badly phrased (what of corporate rights, for example, now so unconstitutionally entrenched within our legal tradition, what of the claims of the other Other, the environment, unendowed with rights or with representation?), and we should everywhere be aware of the problem of political foreclosure, ever tempting us to cynicism, to solipsism. To revisit and resituate my opening remarks on identity, we can suggest, provisionally, that the self may be considered the subjective embodiment in process of an individual, a class, a race, an ethnicity, a region, a church, a political association, a civil institution, a people, a nation, or what have you. The self is that identity-performance that "assumes" power.

By "fantasy," I do not mean to imply that self-empowerment is always and everywhere illusory, for I do not believe that that is the case, nor that it is doomed to remain "prepolitical." The extent to which self-determination is possible is always an open theoretical question and will be relative to—and dependent upon—specific and unique historical circumstances. Moreover, I could not work in the field in which I work without assuming that a little fantasy can go a long, long way. To insist, however mistakenly, that we have taken our destiny into our own hands is the first step to doing so, as with the economic, political, and social struggles of all minorities: the labor movement, the emancipation of women, black or brown or red or yellow power, gay and lesbian rights. Ultimately, of course, and irrevocably, the power of self-naming, the fantasy of self-determination, partakes of a radically democratic impulse that we should be loath to abandon. By fantasy, then, I merely mean that identity formation is fantasmatic, spectral. Individualized emancipation always hinges upon our successful bargaining with the stylized history that enforces its claims upon us. Action (political or otherwise), then identity, is a gaming with ghosts, with history, less a willful forgetting than a shrewd or antic set of negotiations within a marketplace, of which forgetfulness, the maneuver by which we consign our ghosts to oblivion, is merely one bargaining chip, one ace in the hole. We are compelled to reckon with the wraithlike nature of the cultural memories being performatively summoned by a consumerist poetics.

For hauntings entangle progressivist myths and narratives of destiny, insofar as narrative participates in assigning borders, limits, and places to threatening aspects of excess and difference. As Avital Ronell writes, "The questions, as the spirits, that have been raised by the hauntings that have invaded us are not merely a strange fixation of film makers and obsessional neurotics. The relation to a past that, never behind us, is hounding and calling up to us . . . implicates nothing less than an ethics. This ethics—provisional, restless, untried— . . . is an ethics of the haunted" (xviii). Thinking—writing— necessitates a certain kind of steely nostalgia, a shattering, inescapable confrontation with a collective and individual past, however hallucinatory, that will throw the very reality of the present into doubt: "to learn to live *with* ghosts," writes Derrida, "this being-with specters, would also be . . . a *politics of memory*, of inheritance, and of generations" (xviii–xix). Nostalgia has, of course, earned its bad reputation, has always been a primarily conservative alibi; moreover, nostalgia functions today according to the ruthless logic of the marketplace. Yet at each moment, at each juncture, we are solicited. Our own fragile, improvised identities are secured and mobilized by means of a complex cultural and institutional system of associations and references to a necessarily dim, distant, and impossibly idealized past and an accessible, utopian future. As we are sold, as we are sold to, we are promised the power of self-fashioning, relative transcendence.

America is still a big country and getting bigger all the time (in fact, as a cultural phenomenon, I would argue that "America" is stitched across the entire globe). But it is no longer a "spacious" country; "postmodernism" is itself conceived of as the collapse of distance. The postmodern condition is not simply concerned with the burial of a history bound up with a dominant understanding of social norms; it also permits alternative possibilities to emerge, even those possibilities—muted, wraithlike, bloodied—that have been sacrificed. Speaking of the ways in which the ideological collapse of a "literature of dominance" has liberated other tongues, particularly Native American, Vizenor writes:

> The postmodern turn in literature and cultural studies is an invitation to the ruins of representation; the invitation uncovers traces of tribal survivance, trickster discourse, and the remanence of intransitive shadows.
>
> The traces are shadows, shadows, shadows, the natural coherence of archshadows, visions, and memories in heard stories. The postmodern shadows counter paracolonial histories, dickered testimonies, simulations, and the banal essence of consumerism; at the same time, trickster pronouns, transformations, and the shimmers of tribal consciousness are heard in literature. ("Ruins of Representation" 139)

"Spectrality is what makes the present waver," says Jameson reviewing Derrida's *Specters of Marx,* and Derrida insists that we must find ways to conjure, to "learn how to talk with him, with her, how to let them speak or how to give them back speech" (176). Hungry ghosts, the inassimilate, the embodiment—almost—of what has become invisible. In the horror tradition, ghosts are the disembodied dead, solicitous, desirous, who have not finished living, who want our aid in their unfinished business. Otherwise, in the West, ghosts are those improperly buried, unburied, or unceremoniously so, as Morrison indicates. In other traditions, ghosts are spirits, malign, daemonic, or frivolous, and not necessarily the spirits of those who once lived, although they may assume the lineaments of ancestors for purposes of their own. Ghosts, too, symbolize the future that will swamp us. Finally, ghosts return because it is we who want something of them; in this regard it is not so much the dead that haunt the living, but the living that obsessively haunt the dead. The cultural thematics of memory and apocalypse, then, is a ghosting, a haunting of the dead in all of these senses, and the ongoing cultural work of the new century will involve a full reckoning of the unimagined capaciousness of a post-American world. The dead demand that we interrogate the alternative possibilities that seem to have withered and disappeared. In other words, the ghost is a figure by which we might imagine bridges across difference, but also recognize—and honor—that which is lost or sacrificed in any act of exchange or translation or history—that which is abandoned, left behind. The remainder, *that* haunts us, the ghosts of potential, of alternative.

Notes

Introduction

1. While the term is still common in Southern African American vernacular, examples of its use have been collected by folklorists from as far afield as Louisiana, Arkansas, and Tennessee, as well as Texas and Oklahoma. The bluegrass/folk revival band The Pine Hill Haints, describe their music as "Alabama ghost music." In the cult classic *Thunder Road* from 1958, the moonshiner protagonist, Lucas Doolin (Robert Mitchum), is asked by his love interest (Sandra Knight) whether he is afraid of haints. The folklorist Kay L. Cothran cites the centrality of the term in "cracker culture" (340). "Here in Kentucky we mostly refer to them as "ghosts," "hants," or "haints" (1) writes William Lynwood Montell in his collection of Kentucky ghost stories. The fantasy writer Sheree Renée Thomas, in a tribute to Octavia Butler, recalls "haints right out of my grandfather's stories" (351) that haunted her childhood in Memphis and relates them explicitly to descriptions of lynchings. Clearly the term circulated widely, and was put to various uses, although it seems to appear in oral discourse as racial, ethnic, and class power relations are contested and revised. Geraldine Smith-Wright emphasizes that "supernatural tales created by slave owners were deliberately designed to capitalize on slaves' worst fears" (143), but that "Black storytellers shifted their emphasis, often with a great deal of humor, to the prowess and quick thinking of the slave victim" (143).

2. My last keyword search in the MLA International Bibliography for the years 2000–2009 provided 2,595 hits for the keyword *gothic,* with *postmodern* clocking in at 2,012 hits.

3. Clearly, the election of Barack Obama to the presidency of the United States has resurrected these hopes, as is evidenced by his being awarded the Nobel Peace Prize. Even so, and even if our hopes in the progressive dimensions of President

Obama's administration turn out to be well-founded, I think it important and necessary that America's renewed participation in world affairs be multilateral: that the country involves itself in the world as one nation among many rather than as the presumed "leader" of the world.

Chapter 1

1. In *Turncoats, Traitors, and Fellow Travelers,* 70–71.

2. On Allende's "haunted" writing, see in particular Ruth Y. Jenkins's "Authorizing Female Voice and Experience: Ghosts and Spirits in Kingston's *The Woman Warrior* and Allende's *The House of Spirits.*"

3. I am indebted to Frederick Turner for this observation.

4. As Louis S. Gross observes of gothic, "no other genre is so closely linked to the 'feminine' in cultural perception" (91), in part because it "serves as a representation of anxieties concerning the colonization of women's sexuality and the fears of the female metamorphosis free of male control" (91) in the hands of such male writers as Poe or Bram Stoker. In their introduction to *Haunting the House of Fiction,* Lynette Carpenter and Wendy K. Kolmar likewise "claim . . . the existence of a distinctive women's tradition of ghost story writing" (10), pointing out as well that "American women writers with roots in minority cultures seem even more likely to accept the supernatural" (12). The ghost figure undermines the traditionally male prerogative of rationalism, haunted houses fracture the cult of domesticity, serve as a gothic figure for women's captivity, and so forth. What characterizes women's relations to ghosts, typically, is sympathy. One factor that distinguishes women's writing in the genre is that in such works "women characters realize their commonality with the ghostly women and children they encounter" (14).

Chapter 2

1. On the mythic quest for communal identity in *Song of Solomon,* see Valerie Smith's "The Quest for and Discovery of Identity in Toni Morrison's *Song of Solomon.*" For an elaboration of the ways in which Morrison utilizes and challenges the heroic paradigm, see Linda Krumholz's "Dead Teachers: Rituals of Manhood and Rituals of Reading in *Song of Solomon.*"

2. In a series of essays by various writers and critics, the important volume *History and Memory in African-American Culture,* edited by Genevieve Fabre and Robert O'Meally relates Nora's essay to a variety of aspects of African American history, culture, and literature.

3. On the various sorts of languages used in the novel and how they typify

class, gender, and cultural distinctions, see Corinne Dale's "The Power of Language in Lee Smith's *Oral History*"; on gender policing as an aspect of regulations of insiders and outsiders, see David Reynolds's "Customary Ritual and Male Rites of Passage in Lee Smith's *Oral History*."

4. See the preamble to book 2 of *Let Us Now Praise Famous Men.*

5. Several critics have commented on the relationship between commercialization and exoticism in Smith's novel. For Margaret D. Bauer, for example, the novel charts the destruction of a southern Appalachian community by the forces of patriarchy and capitalism, although she concedes that "the legend of Dory ultimately predominates" (37); I would add as well that, in Smith's novel, women characters are both victims and enforcers of patriarchy. For Nancy C. Parrish, the theme park Ghostland points to Appalachian "quaintness commodified" (45); the cultural survival of societies that have evaporated under the pressures of an accelerating modernization can survive only by "haunting" their own commodification, the only ways in which they circulate today.

6. Though I have accentuated the positive throughout my reading, Janelle Collins is correct to argue that the conclusion is ambiguous, an open question, that the "explosion signifies both a utopian and a dystopian vision" (45), depending on the ways in which characters and readers act upon their perceptions and understandings.

7. As I write, ex–Detroit mayor Kwame Kilpatrick awaits sentencing for his involvement in corruption, sex scandals, obstruction of justice, and assault.

8. On American frontier gothic and D. H. Lawrence, see the editors' introduction to *Frontier Gothic: Terror and Wonder at the Frontier in American Literature,* edited by David Mogen, Scott P. Sanders, and Joanne B. Karpinski. On violence and the frontier see Richard Slotkin's remarkable trilogy, *Regeneration through Violence, The Fatal Environment,* and *Gunfighter Nation,* which traces this myth through from the foundings of the nation up to contemporary times.

9. On Lynch's *Blue Velvet,* see Laura Mulvey's "The Pre-Oedipal Father: The Gothicism of *Blue Velvet*" in *Modern Gothic: A Reader,* edited by Victor Sage and Allan Lloyd-Smith. A more general discussion of Lynch's work in a gothic context can be found in the final chapter of Richard Davenport-Hines's *Gothic: Four Hundred Years of Excess, Horror, Evil and Ruin.*

10. Yet Edmundson's argument also participates in this dread: He takes time out to insist that demands for liberation have "often grown more simple minded and self-righteous over time" (64), a judgment that only suggests he is increasingly out of touch. Many demands are simplistic and self righteous, but so they have always been. But they do not look that way when we share them: They look like a simple question of justice. After all, was not the protest of American imperial involvement in southeast Asia simplistic and self-righteous? Was not aboli-

tionism? Was not the suffrage movement? Protests against child labor or on behalf of workers' right? To their enemies, progressive movements always seem simplistic and self-righteous, which does not make the causes they espouse any less just.

Chapter 3

1. As Doug Rossinow points out, "Reagan revisionism is hard upon us" (1279). A spate of new and highly ambivalent histories have appeared in the past few years, aiming to assess the social and cultural history of the decade as well as the achievements and failures of the administration. For a thoughtful review of the extent to which these works resist the triumphant narrative of Reaganism, see Rossinow's review of these works, "Talking Points Memo" in *American Quarterly.*

2. See my *Turncoats, Traitors, and Fellow Travelers.*

3. This is only partly true of Vizenor, which may be why it is the only one that has garnered much critical attention.

4. In response to criticisms from feminist readers, Vizenor bowdlerized the second edition slightly, changing passages in the "frame" narrative that opens the book.

5. Vizenor's collection of theoretical essays, *Manifest Manners: Narratives of Postindian Survivance,* originally published in 1994 and reissued by the University of Nebraska Press in 1999, remains the best introduction to his thinking. Kimberly M. Blaeser's 1994 *Gerald Vizenor: Writing in the Oral Tradition* is an indispensable guide to his fiction.

6. For an outline of the differences and similarities between Silko's understanding of the aboriginal revolutionary imagination and Baudrillard's, see in particular Ami M. Regier's "Material Meeting Points of Self and Other: Fetish Discourses and Leslie Marmon Silko's Evolving Conception of Cross-Cultural Narrative." As Regier points out, Silko largely renounces Baudrillard's Eurocentric perspective: She will neither abandon the demand for the return of the lands, nor is she particularly concerned about the effects, viral or otherwise, of Indians upon Europeans.

7. Despite its obvious topicality and the various ways in which the overarching themes of the book—the status of faith and its enduring appeal in a supposedly secular society and the problem of divine intervention or retribution—echo public discussions emerging in the aftermath of the September 11 attacks, *City of God* has received almost no lengthy critical consideration to date.

8. Consider, for example, the 2005 effort to get Sharia law recognized within the secular courts of Ontario, Canada. Similarly, the long histories of civil dis-

obedience, pacifism, jihad, abortion-clinic bombing, and the like, draws spiritual sustenance from the appeal to a "higher law" than that imposed by national courts. Ironically, secular law recognizes its own limitations when it grants special exemptions to Quakers or to conscientious objectors.

9. On the relation of Doctorow to the postmodern, see in particular John Williams's *Fiction as False Document: The Reception of E. L. Doctorow in the Postmodern Age*. Doctorow, Williams astutely points out, "has mirrored the era's skepticism about the objectivity of history, its preoccupation with linguistic construction of reality and the human self, its fascination with popular culture, its irreverence, and its consuming anxiety over the clash of diverse cultures" (14–15). The inescapable political ferocity of this last aspect of the postmodern condition, coupled with the emerging institutional power of religious fundamentalisms of all stripes globally, suggests that many of the theoretical and aesthetic discussions of postmodernism that circulated so widely in the 1980s and '90s had only the thinnest grasp of with what—and whom—they were reckoning.

10. Relativism is at best a frustrating misnomer to describe the postmodern condition as Lyotard or others have conceived it. Relativism does not, in fact, imply that all moral perspectives are equivalent and thereby strip us of the capacity to credibly distinguish among them; quite the reverse. Consider, for example, terms that are inarguably relative, like size. A cat is "large" relative to an ant, but "small" relative to a whale. This does not, however, imply that cats, ants, and whales are all the same size. Indeed, relativism is the most powerful ethical technology available for making compelling assessments of difference in a world without any guarantees of such absolutes measures as "good" or "evil." Relativism remains, however, an abstract moral technology. When put in practice in the world, inevitably, such assessments are always a function of rhetoric and power.

11. For a fuller discussion of Benjamin's theorization of mythic and divine violence, see my *Raids on Human Consciousness*, 63–65.

12. This is true, I think, despite Osama bin Laden's claims that the attacks were protest against American military presence in Saudi Arabia. The ongoing fighting in Iraq and Afghanistan seem to constitute guerilla warfare in a now fairly traditional sense. It is more difficult to assess the attacks in Madrid and London, which seem acts guided by a logic of revenge or retribution, rather than, in Benjamin's sense, mythic acts of violence that instantiate a new order.

13. Baudrillard's own intriguing comments on the World Trade Center and Pentagon attacks hinge, curiously enough, on an inversion of his usual logic. What is so provoking about the attacks of September 11, he argues, is that they in fact *did* take place! That is, they assumed the rhetorical and affective status of an event whose consequences render it "genuine" in ways that none of the media generated virtual or pseudo events of the past few years can equal. In keeping

with Baudrillard, we might say that 9/11 is not so much real, perhaps, as relevant. The attacks matter in profound ways: "With the attacks on the World Trade
Center of New York, we might even be said to have before us the absolute event,
the 'mother' of all events, the pure event uniting within itself all the events that
have never taken place" (3–4).

14. According to Gloria Goodale in the September 21 edition of the *Christian
Science Monitor,* the Schwarzenegger film *Collateral Damage; Big Trouble,* a Tim
Allen comedy; Jackie Chan's *Nosebleed;* and a trailer for *Spiderman* were pulled,
rewritten, or delayed as an immediate response to the attacks.

Conclusion

1. See in particular Louis S. Gross, *Redefining the American Gothic: From
Wieland to Day of the Dead,* Brian Atteby, *The Fantasy Tradition in American Literature: From Irving to Le Guin,* Justin D. Edwards, *Gothic Passages: Racial Am-
biguity and the American Gothic,* and *The Haunted Dusk: American Supernatural
Fiction, 1820–1920,* edited by Howard Kerr, John W. Crowley, and Charles L.
Crow. The classic interrogation of American gothic remains Leslie A. Fiedler's
Love and Death in the American Novel, wherein he notes at length how "in our
most enduring books, the cheapjack machinery of the gothic novel is called on
to represent the hidden blackness of human soul and human society" (27). Alan
Lloyd-Smith's *American Gothic Fiction: An Introduction* is an excellent book for
beginning students.

2. I began this project, initially, because I could not help but notice how
many ghosts turned up in the contemporary fiction I was teaching and reading,
in books that were worlds apart generically, stylistically, and temperamentally.

3. For a classic account of Griffith's formal achievement, see chapter 3 of
David A. Cook's *A History of Narrative Film.*

4. On the ongoing public dilemmas and struggles over the variety of ways in
which Griffith's epic can be interpreted, see "*The Birth of a Nation:* Reconsidering
Its Reception," chapter 7 of Janet Staiger's *Interpreting Film.*

5. Curiously (or perhaps not so), in both Scorsese's version and the original
1961 film, directed by J. Lee Thompson, the character of Max Cady, though played
by white actors, assumes traditionally black attributes. In each case racial difference is deflected onto class anxiety and the dread of the white Other. In the
original, filmed during the growth of the civil rights movement, Cady (Robert
Mitchum) plays a sexual predator who is thereby deemed unworthy of "civil
rights," although Sam Bowden (Gregory Peck) eventually forswears the temp-
tations of vigilante justice in favor of the essential justice of the legal system. By
1991, this system is itself portrayed as hopelessly corrupt, and the dialectics of

race and class are more subtle. Cady (Robert De Niro) is deliberately positioned as poor white: "from the hills, pentecostal crackers." He repeatedly insists that he is "just as good as" Bowden, and thus can rightfully have what Bowden (Nick Nolte) possesses (car, home, social position, wife, family). Bowden, a representative of the "New South" is corrupt and castrated. He cheats on his clients and his wife and is thereby unworthy of his status. His manhood must consequently be tested in a highly staged "trial" with Cady; he must prove they are not of the same blood. The film raises the specter of miscegenation (Cady's right to proprietorship over the domain of the New South) only to ultimately exorcise it. Bowden is the "better" man. Again, white womanhood is presented as typically under assault, as the prize to be won, although in this "postfeminist" film, women achieve a carefully controlled measure of agency. Danielle Bowden (Juliette Lewis) asserts control over the narrative; she tells her own coming-of-age story. As the object of the camera's fascination, she is portrayed as both innocent and sexually aggressive, as the childlike victim of Cady's advances and his seducer.

6. I am indebted to conversations with Irina Novikova for this insight.

Works Cited

Agee, James, and Walker Evans. *Let Us Now Praise Famous Men.* 1941. Boston: Houghton Mifflin, 1988. Print.

Allende, Isabel. *My Invented Country: A Nostalgic Journey through Chile.* Trans. Margaret Sayers Peden. New York: HarperCollins, 2003. Print.

Anderson, Eric Gary. "Black Atlanta: An Ecosocial Approach to Narratives of the Atlanta Child Murders." *PMLA* 122.1 (2007): 194–209. Print.

Arkush, R. David, and Leo K. Lee, eds. *Land without Ghosts: Chinese Impressions of America from the Mid-Nineteenth Century to the Present.* Berkeley: U of California P, 1989. Print.

Artéaga, Alfred, ed., *An Other Tongue: Nation and Ethnicity from the Linguistic Borderlands.* Durham: Duke UP, 1994. Print.

Atteby, Brian. *The Fantasy Tradition in American Literature: From Irving to Le Guin.* Bloomington: Indiana UP, 1980. Print.

Auster, Paul. *Ghosts. The New York Trilogy.* New York: Penguin, 1994. Print.

Baldwin, James. *The Evidence of Things Not Seen.* New York: Holt, Rinehart and Winston, 1985. Print.

Bambara, Toni Cade. *Deep Sightings and Rescue Missions: Fiction, Essays, and Conversations.* New York: Pantheon, 1996. Print.

———. *The Salt Eaters.* New York: Random House, 1980. Print.

———. *Those Bones Are Not My Child.* New York: Pantheon, 1999. Print.

Barnett, Louise K., and James L. Thorson, eds. *Leslie Marmon Silko: A Collection of Critical Essays.* Albuquerque: U of New Mexico P, 1999. Print.

Baudrillard, Jean. *The Intelligence of Evil, or the Lucidity Pact.* Trans. Chris Turner. Oxford: Berg, 2005. Print.

Bauer, Margaret D. "No Mere Endurance Here: The Prevailing Woman's Voice in Lee Smith's *Oral History.*" *Pembroke Magazine* 33 (2001): 59–68. Print.

———. *The Transparency of Evil: Essays on Extreme Phenomena*. Trans. James
Benedict. London: Verso, 1993. Print.

Belau, Linda. "Introduction. Remembering, Repeating, and Working-Through:
Trauma and the Limit of Knowledge." *Topologies of Trauma*. Ed. Linda Belau
and Petar Ramadanovic. New York: Other, 2002. Print.

Benjamin, Walter. "Critique of Violence." *Reflections*. Trans. Edmund Jephcott.
New York: Schocken, 1986. 277–300. Print.

———. "Surrealism. The Last Snapshot of the European Intelligentsia." *Reflections: Essays, Aphorisms, Autobiographical Writings*. Trans. Edmund Jephcott. Ed. Peter Demetz. New York: Harcourt Brace Jovanovich, 1978. 177–
192. Print.

Bergland, Renée L. *The National Uncanny: Indian Ghosts and American Subjects*.
Hanover: UP of New England, 2000. Print.

Bhabha, Homi K. "DissemiNation: Time, Narrative and the Margins of the Modern Nation." *The Location of Culture*. London: Routledge, 1994. 139–170. Print.

Bianco, Jamie Skye. "Zones of Morbidity" *Rhizomes: Cultural Studies in Emerging Knowledges* 8 (Spring 2004): 34 par. Web. 26 Jan. 2008. <http://www
.rhizomes.net/issue8/index.html>.

Blaeser, Kimberly M. *Gerald Vizenor: Writing in the Oral Tradition*. Norman: U
of Oklahoma P, 1994. Print.

Blanchot, Maurice. *The Writing of the Disaster*. Trans. Ann Smock. Lincoln: U of
Nebraska P, 1986. Print.

Bone, Martyn. "Capitalist Abstraction and the Body Politics of Place in Toni Cade
Bambara's *Those Bones Are Not My Child*." *Journal of American Studies* 37
(2003): 229–246. Print.

Botting, Fred. *Gothic*. London: Routledge, 1996. Print.

Boyle, T. Coraghessen. *World's End*. 1987. New York: Penguin, 1990. Print.

Brogan, Kathleen. *Cultural Haunting: Ghosts in Recent American Literature*. Charlottesville: UP of Virginia, 1998. Print.

Brown, Charles Brockden. *Wieland, or, The Transformation: An American Tale*.
1798. Garden City, NJ: Anchor, 1969. Print.

Burchell, Sonya Smith. "Female Characterization in Lee Smith's *Oral History*: Su-
perstition, Sexuality, and Traditional Roles." *North Carolina Folklore Journal*
42.2 (1995): 105–112. Print.

Carpenter, Lynette, and Wendy K. Kolmar. *Haunting the House of Fiction: Feminist Perspectives on Ghosts Stories by American Women*. Knoxville: U of Tennessee P, 1991. Print.

Carter, Angela. *American Ghosts and Old World Wonders*. London: Chatto and
Windus, 1993. Print.

Cazdyn, Eric. "Disaster, Crisis, Revolution." *The South Atlantic Quarterly* 6.4 (Fall 2007): 647–662. Print.

Chávez-Candelaria, Cordelia. "Différance and the Discourse of 'Community' in Writings by and about the Ethnic Other(s)." Artéaga. 185–202. Print.

Collins, Janelle. "Generating Power: Fission, Fusion, and Postmodern Politics in Bambara's *The Salt Eaters.*" *MELUS* 21.2 (Summer 1996): 35–47. Print.

Cook, David A. *A History of Narrative Film.* 3rd ed. New York: Norton, 1996. Print.

Cothran, Kay L. "Talking Trash in the Okefenokee Swamp Rim, Georgia." *Journal of American Folklore* 87.346 (1974): 340–356. Print.

Dale, Corinne. "The Power of Language in Lee Smith's *Oral History.*" *Southern Quarterly* 28 (Winter 1990): 21–34. Print.

Dark, Larry, ed. *The Literary Ghost: Great Contemporary Ghost Stories.* New York: Atlantic Monthly P, 1991. Print.

Davenport-Hines, Richard. *Gothic: Four Hundred Years of Excess, Horror, Evil and Ruin.* New York: Farrar, Straus, and Giroux, 1998. Print.

Davis, Colin. *Haunted Subjects: Deconstruction, Psychoanalysis and the Return of the Dead.* New York: Palgrave Macmillan, 2007. Print.

Deleuze, Gilles. *Negotiations, 1972–1990.* Trans. Martin Joughin. New York: Columbia UP, 1995. Print.

——, and Félix Guattari. *Kafka: Toward a Minor Literature.* Trans. Dana Polan. Minneapolis: U of Minnesota P, 1986. Print.

——. *A Thousand Plateaus: Capitalism and Schizophrenia.* Trans. Brian Massumi. Minneapolis: U of Minnesota P, 1987. Print.

Derrida, Jacques. *Specters of Marx: The State of the Debt, the Work of Mourning, and the New International.* Trans. Peggy Kamuf. New York: Routledge, 1994. Print.

Dettlinger, Chet, and Jeff Prugh. *The List.* Atlanta: Philmay Enterprises, 1984. Print.

Doctorow, E. L. *City of God.* New York: Random House, 2000. Print.

——. "The Politics of God" *Reporting the Universe.* Cambridge: Harvard UP, 2003. 89–98. Print.

——. "Texts That Are Sacred, Texts That Are Not." *Reporting the Universe.* 51–56. Print.

——. *The Waterworks.* New York: Random House, 1994. Print.

Du Bois, W. E. B. *Black Reconstruction in America: An Essay toward a History of the Part which Black Folk Played in the Attempt to Reconstruct Democracy in America, 1860–1880.* 1935. Cleveland: World, 1960. Print.

——. *The Souls of Black Folk.* 1903. *W. E. B. Du Bois: Writings.* Ed. Nathan Huggins. New York: Library of America, 1986. 357–548. Print.

Eagleton, Terry. "Ideology and Literary Form." 1976. *The Eagleton Reader.* Ed. Stephan Regan. Oxford: Blackwell, 1988. 171–93. Print.

Edmundson, Mark. *Nightmare on Main Street: Angels, Sadomasochism, and the Culture of Gothic.* Cambridge: Harvard UP, 1997. Print.

Edwards, Justin D. *Gothic Passages: Racial Ambiguity and the American Gothic.* Iowa City: U of Iowa P, 2003. Print.

Eisinger, Peter K. *The Politics of Displacement: Racial and Ethnic Transition in Three American Cities.* New York: Academic Press, 1980. Print.

Ellison, Ralph. *Invisible Man.* 1952. New York: Vintage, 1980. Print.

———. *Shadow and Act.* New York: Random House, 1966. Print.

Erdrich, Louise. *Tracks.* New York: Holt, 1988. Print.

Eyerman, Ron. *Cultural Trauma: Slavery and the Formation of African-American Identity.* Cambridge: Cambridge UP, 2001. Print.

Fabre, Genevieve, and Robert O'Meally, eds. *History and Memory in African American Culture.* New York: Oxford UP, 1994. Print.

Fischer, Michael M. J. "Ethnicity and the Post-Modern Arts of Memory." *Writing Culture: The Poetics and Politics of Ethnography.* Ed. James Clifford and George E. Marcus. Berkeley: U of California P, 1986. 194–233. Print.

Fiedler, Leslie A. *Love and Death in the American Novel.* Rev. ed. New York: Stein and Day, 1966. Print.

Fried Green Tomatoes. Dir. Jon Avnet. Universal, 1991. Film.

Frisch, Michael H. "The Memory of History." *Presenting the Past: Essays on History and the Public.* Ed. Susan Porter Benson, Stephen Brier, and Roy Rosenzweig. Philadelphia: Temple UP, 1986. 5–17. Print.

Gilman, Charlotte Perkins. "The Yellow Wallpaper." 1892. *The Charlotte Perkins Gilman Reader.* Ed. Ann J. Lane. New York: Pantheon, 1980. Print.

Girard, René. *The Scapegoat.* Trans. Yvonne Freccero. Baltimore: Johns Hopkins UP, 1986. Print.

Goddu, Teresa A. *Gothic America: Narrative, History, and Nation.* New York: Columbia UP, 1997. Print.

Goodale, Gloria. "After Attacks, Will Hollywood Change Its Ways?" *Christian Science Monitor* 21 (Sept. 2001): 15. Print.

Gordon, Avery F. *Ghostly Matters: Haunting and the Sociological Imagination.* Minneapolis: U of Minnesota P, 1997. Print.

Griffith, D. W., dir. *The Birth of a Nation.* Epoch, 1915. Film.

Gross, Louis S. *Redefining the American Gothic: from Wieland to Day of the Dead.* Ann Arbor: U.M.I. Research P, 1989. Print.

Guth, Deborah. "A Blessing and a Burden: The Relation to the Past in *Sula, Song of Solomon,* and *Beloved.*" *Toni Morrison Double Issue.* Ed. Nancy J. Peterson. Spec. issue of *Modern Fiction Studies* 39.3–4 (1993): 575–96. Print.

Hardt, Michael. "The Politics of Love and Evil." Ioan Davies Memorial Lecture. York University, Toronto. 15 Sept. 2005. Lecture.

Hardt, Michael, and Antonio Negri. *Empire*. Cambridge: Harvard UP, 2000. Print.

Harpham, Geoffrey Galt. "E. L. Doctorow and the Technology of Narrative." *Modern Critical Views: E. L. Doctorow*. Ed. Harold Bloom. Philadelphia: Chelsea House, 2002. 27–50. Print.

Hawthorne, Nathaniel. "Preface." *The Marble Faun. The Riverside Edition of the Complete Works*. Vol. VI. Boston: Houghton Mifflin, 1849. Print.

Herman, Judith Lewis. *Trauma and Recovery*. New York: Basic, 1992. Print.

Highsmith, Patricia. *Tales of Natural and Unnatural Catastrophes*. 1987. New York: Atlantic Monthly P, 1994. Print.

Hopkins, Pauline. *The Magazine Novels of Pauline Hopkins*. Ed. Hazel Carby. New York: Oxford UP, 1990. Print.

Hull, Gloria T. (Akasha). "What It Is I Think She's Doing Anyhow: A Reading of Toni Cade Bambara's *The Salt Eaters*." *Home Girls: A Black Feminist Anthology*. Ed. Barbara Smith. New Brunswick: Rutgers UP, 2000. 124–142. Print.

Huntington, Samuel P. *Who Are We: The Challenges to America's National Identity*. New York: Simon and Schuster, 2004. Print.

Irr, Caren. "The Timeliness of *Almanac of the Dead*, or a Postmodern Rewriting of Radical Fiction." Barnett and Thorson. 223–244. Print.

Jacoby, Russell. *The End of Utopia: Politics and Culture in an Age of Apathy*. New York: Basic, 1999. Print.

James, Henry. "The Jolly Corner." *The Tales of Henry James: The Texts of His Stories, The Author on His Craft, Background and Criticism*. Ed. Christof Wegelin. New York: Norton, 1984. 313–340. Print.

———. *The Turn of the Screw*. 1898. New York: Penguin, 1987. Print.

Jameson, Fredric. *Postmodernism, or The Cultural Logic of Late Capitalism*. London: Verso, 1991. Print.

Jenkins, Ruth Y. "Authorizing Female Voice and Experience: Ghosts and Spirits in Kingston's *The Woman Warrior* and Allende's *The House of Spirits*." *MELUS* 19.3 (Fall 1999): 61–74. Print.

Kammen, Michael. *Mystic Chords of Memory: The Transformation of Tradition in American Culture*. New York: Knopf, 1991. Print.

Kelley, Margot Anne. "'Damballah Is the First Law of Thermodynamics': Modes of Access to Toni Cade Bambara's *The Salt Eaters*." *African American Review* 27.3 (1993): 479–493. Print.

Kennedy, William. *Ironweed*. New York: Viking, 1983. Print.

Kerr, Howard, John W. Crowley, and Charles L. Crow, eds. *The Haunted Dusk: American Supernatural Fiction, 1820–1920*. Athens: U of Georgia P, 1983. Print.

Kincaid, Jamaica. *Annie John*. New York: Farrar, Straus, and Giroux, 1985. Print.

———. *At the Bottom of the River.* 1984. New York: Plume, 1992. Print.

———. *The Autobiography of My Mother.* New York: Farrar, Straus, and Giroux, 1996. Print.

———. *My Brother.* New York: Farrar, Straus, and Giroux, 1997. Print.

Kingston, Maxine Hong. *China Men.* New York: Knopf, 1980. Print.

———. *The Woman Warrior: Memoirs of a Girlhood Among Ghosts.* New York: Knopf, 1976. Print.

Klein, Naomi. *The Shock Doctrine: The Rise and Fall of Disaster Capitalism.* New York: Henry Holt, 2007. Print.

Krumholz, Linda. "Dead Teachers: Rituals of Manhood and Rituals of Reading in *Song of Solomon.*" *MFS Modern Fiction Studies* 39.3–4 (1993): 551–574. Print.

Kunstler, James Howard. *The City in Mind: Notes on the Urban Condition.* New York: Free Press, 2002. Print.

Kurtz, Stanley. "Those 9/11 Songs: Are You with Springsteen or Keith?" *NRO: National Review Online* 27 Aug. 2002. Web. 30 Sept. 2008. <http://www.nationalreview.com/kurtz/kurtz082702.asp>.

Lawrence, D. H. *Studies in Classic American Literature.* New York: Doubleday/Anchor, 1955. Print.

Lloyd-Smith, Allan. *American Gothic Fiction: An Introduction.* New York: Continuum, 2004. Print.

———. "Postmodernism/Gothicism." Sage and Lloyd-Smith. 6–19. Print.

Lurie, Alison. *Women and Ghosts.* London: Minerva, 1994. Print.

Lynch, David, dir. *Blue Velvet.* Perf. Isabella Rossellini. De Laurentis Entertainment, 1986. Film.

Lyotard, Jean-François. *The Differend: Phrases in Dispute.* Trans. Georges van den Abbeele. Minneapolis: U of Minnesota P, 1988. Print.

———, and Jean-Loup Thébaud. *Just Gaming.* Trans. Wlad Godzich. Minneapolis: U of Minnesota P, 1985. Print.

Martin, Robert K., and Eric Savoy, eds. *American Gothic: New Interventions in a National Narrative.* Iowa City: U of Iowa P, 1998. Print.

Masse, Michelle A. *In the Name of Love: Masochism and the Gothic.* Ithaca: Cornell UP, 1992. Print.

Michaud, Marilyn. *Republicanism and the American Gothic.* Cardiff: U of Wales P, 2009. Print.

Mogen, David, Scott P. Sanders, and Joanne B. Karpinski, eds. *Frontier Gothic: Terror and Wonder at the Frontier in American Literature.* London: Associated University Presses, 1993. Print.

Montell, William Lynwood. *Kentucky Ghosts.* Lexington: UP of Kentucky, 1994. Print.

Morrison, Toni. *Beloved.* New York: Knopf, 1987. Print.

——. "Interview." *The Paris Review* 35 (1993): 82–125. Print.

——. "Living Memory: A Conversation with Miriam Horn," *City Limits* 31 Mar.–7 Apr. 1988: 10–11. Print.

——. "Memory, Creation, Writing." *Thought: A Review of Culture and Ideas.* 59.235 (1984): 385–390. Print.

——. "The Official Story: Dead Man Golfing." Morrison and Lacour. vii–xxvii. Print.

——. *Playing in the Dark: Whiteness and the American Literary Imagination.* Cambridge: Harvard UP, 1992. Print.

——. "The Site of Memory." *Inventing the Truth: The Art and Craft of Memoir.* Ed. William Zinsser. Boston: Houghton Mifflin, 1984. Print.

——. *Song of Solomon.* New York: Knopf, 1977. Print.

——, and Claudia Brodsky Lacour, eds. *The Birth of a Nation'hood: Gaze, Script, and Spectacle in the O. J. Simpson Case.* New York: Pantheon, 1997. Print.

——, and Gloria Naylor. "A Conversation." *The Southern Review* 21.3 (1985): 567–593. Print.

Mulvey, Laura. "The Pre-Oedipal Father: The Gothicism of *Blue Velvet.*" Sage and Lloyd-Smith. 38–57. Print.

Nora, Pierre. "Between History and Memory: Les Lieux de Mémoire." Trans. Mark Roudebush. *History and Memory in African-American Culture.* Ed. Geneviève Fabre and O'Meally. New York: Oxford UP, 1994. 284–300. Print.

O'Connor, Flannery. "The Grotesque in Southern Fiction." *Mystery and Manners.* New York: Farrar, Straus, and Giroux, 1969. Print.

Olsen, Tillie. *Silences.* 1978. New York: Pell, 1983. Print.

Ondaatje, Michael. *Anil's Ghost.* New York: Knopf, 2000. Print.

Owens, Louis. Afterword. *Bearheart.* By Gerald Vizenor. Print.

——. *Other Destinies: Understanding the American Indian Novel.* Norman: U of Oklahoma P, 1992. Print.

Parrish, Nancy C. "Ghostland: Tourism in Lee Smith's *Oral History.*" *Southern Quarterly* 32.2 (Winter 1994): 37–47. Print.

Paz, Octavio. "Mexico and the United States." *The Labyrinth of Solitude.* 2nd ed. New York: Grove, 1985. Print.

Pearlman, Mickey, ed. *American Women Writing Fiction: Memory, Identity, Family, Space.* Lexington: UP of Kentucky, 1989. Print.

Poe, Edgar Allan. "The Philosophy of Composition." *The Complete Works of Edgar Allan Poe.* Vol. 14. *Essays and Miscellanies.* Ed. James A. Harrison. New York: AMS Press, 1965. Print.

Ramadanovic, Petar. "In the Future . . . : On Trauma and Literature." *Topologies of Trauma: Essays on the Limits of Knowledge and Memory.* Ed. Linda Belau and Petar Ramadanovic. New York: Other, 2002. 179–209. Print.

Redding, Arthur. *Raids on Human Consciousness: Writing, Anarchism, and Violence.* Columbia: U of South Carolina P, 1998. Print.

———. *Turncoats, Traitors, and Fellow Travelers: Culture and Politics of the Early Cold War.* Jackson: UP of Mississippi, 2008. Print.

Regier, Ami M. "Material Meeting Points of Self and Other: Fetish Discourses and Leslie Marmon Silko's Evolving Conception of Cross-Cultural Narrative." Barnett and Thorson. 185–206. Print.

Reynolds, David. "Customary Ritual and Male Rites of Passage in Lee Smith's *Oral History.*" *North Carolina Folklore Journal* 42.2 (1995): 113–122. Print.

Rich, Adrienne. "What Ghosts Can Say." *A Change of World. Collected Early Poems, 1950–1970.* New York: Norton, 1993. Print.

———. "When We Dead Awaken: Writing as Re-Vision." *On Lies, Secrets and Silence: Selected Prose 1966–1978.* New York: Norton, 1979. Print.

Roach, Joseph. *Cities of the Dead: Circum-Atlantic Performance.* New York: Columbia UP, 1996. Print.

Rodriguez, Francisco Collado. "The Profane becomes Sacred: Escaping Eclecticism in Doctorow's City of God" *Atlantis, revista de la Asociación Espanola de Estudios Anglo-Norteamericanos* 24.1 (June 2002): 59–70. Print.

Ronell, Avital. *Dictations: On Haunted Writing.* 1986. Lincoln: U of Nebraska P, 1993. Print.

Rossinow, Doug. "Talking Points Memo." *American Quarterly* 59.4 (Dec. 2007): 1279–1289. Print.

Sage, Victor, and Allan Lloyd-Smith, eds. *Modern Gothic: A Reader.* Manchester: Manchester UP, 1996. Print.

San Juan, E., Jr. "Problematizing Multiculturalism and the 'Common Culture.'" *Melus* 19.2 (Summer 1994): 59–83. Print.

Sandoval, Cheva. *Methodology of the Oppressed.* Minneapolis: U of Minnesota P, 2000. Print.

Savoy, Eric. "The Face of the Tenant: A Theory of American Gothic." Martin and Savoy. 3–19. Print.

———. The Rise of American Gothic." *The Cambridge Companion to Gothic Fiction.* Ed. Eric Hogle. Cambridge: Cambridge UP, 2002. 167–188. Print.

Scarry, Elaine. *The Body in Pain.* New York: Oxford UP, 1987. Print.

Schama, Simon. "History and the Literary Imagination." Public Lecture. Wolfson College, Oxford. 29 May 1997. Lecture.

Scorsese, Martin, dir. *Cape Fear.* Perf. Nick Nolte, Robert De Niro, and Juliette Lewis. Universal, 1991. Film.

Sexton, Anne. "The Ghost." Dark. 225–229. Print.

Shakespeare, William. *The Tragedy of Hamlet, Prince of Denmark.* Ed. Barbara A. Mowat and Paul Werstone. New York: Washington Square, 1993. Print.

Silko, Leslie Marmon. *Almanac of the Dead.* 1991. New York: Viking Penguin, 1992. Print.

Slotkin, Richard. *The Fatal Environment: The Myth of the Frontier in the Age of Industrialization, 1800–1890.* New York: Atheneum, 1985. Print.

———. *Gunfighter Nation: The Myth of the Frontier in Twentieth-Century America.* New York: Harper Perennial, 1992. Print.

———. *Regeneration through Violence: The Mythology of the American Frontier.* Middletown, CN: Wesleyan UP, 1973. Print.

Smith, Daniel W. "Introduction: 'A Life of Pure Immanence': Deleuze's 'Critique et Clinique' Project." *Essays Critical and Clinical.* Trans. Daniel Smith and Michael A. Greco. Ed. Gilles Deleuze. Minneapolis: U of Minnesota P, 1997. Print.

Smith, Lee. *Oral History.* 1983. New York: Ballantine, 2003. Print.

Smith, Valerie. "The Quest for and Discovery of Identity in Toni Morrison's *Song of Solomon.*" In *Toni Morrison's Song of Solomon: A Casebook.* Ed. Jan Furman. Oxford: Oxford UP, 2003. 27-41. Print.

Smith-Wright, Geraldine. "In Spite of the Klan: Ghosts in the Fiction of Black Women Writers." Carpenter and Kolmar. 142–165. Print.

Sollors, Werner. *Beyond Ethnicity: Consent and Descent in American Culture.* New York: Oxford UP, 1986. Print.

Sonser, Anna. *A Passion for Consumption: The Gothic Novel in America.* Bowling Green, OH: Bowling Green State UP, 2001. Print.

Spielberg, Steven, prod. *Poltergeist.* Dir. Tobe Hooper. MGM/United Artists, 1982. Film.

Spillers, Hortense J. "Introduction: Who Cuts the Border? Some Readings on 'America.'" *Comparative American Identities: Race, Sex, and Nationality in the Modern Text.* Ed. Hortense Spillers. New York: Routledge, 1991. Print.

———. "Mama's Baby, Papa's Maybe: An American Grammar Book." *Diacritics* 17.2 (Summer 1987): 65–81. Print.

Spooner, Catherine. *Contemporary Gothic.* London: Reaktion Books, 2006. Print.

Staiger, Janet. *Interpreting Film: Studies in the Historical Reception of American Cinema.* Princeton: Princeton UP, 1992. Print.

Taylor, Carol Anne. "Postmodern Disconnection and the Archive of Bones: Toni Cade Bambara's Last Work." *Novel: A Forum on Fiction,* 35.2/3 (Spring/Summer 2002): 258–280. Print.

Thunder Road. Perf. Robert Mitchum. United Artists, 1958. Film.

Thomas, Sheree Renée. "Praisesong on the Passage of a Brilliant Star from a Dreamer Below." *Callaloo* 29.2 (2006): 340–356. Print.

Thompson, J. Lee, dir. *Cape Fear.* Perf. Robert Mitchum and Gregory Peck. Universal, 1961. Film.

Tocqueville, Alexis de. *Democracy in America.* Vol. 2. 1840. New York: Vintage, 1990. Print.

Tokarczyk, Michelle M. *E. L. Doctorow's Skeptical Commitment.* New York: Peter Lang, 2000. Print.

Vaid, Krishna Baldev. "The Jolly Corner." *Tales of Henry James: The Texts of His Stories, The Author on His Craft, Background and Criticism.* Ed. Christ of Wegelin. New York: Norton, 1984. 484–487. Print.

Veeder, William. "The Nurture of the Gothic, or How Can a Text Be Both Popular and Subversive?" Martin and Savoy. 20–39. Print.

Vickroy, Laurie. *Trauma and Survival in Contemporary Fiction.* Charlottesville: U of Virginia P, 2002. Print.

Vizenor, Gerald. *Bearheart: The Heirship Chronicles.* Minneapolis: University of Minnesota P, 1990. Print.

———. *Manifest Manners: Narratives of Postindian Survivance.* 1994. Lincoln: U of Nebraska P, 1999. Print.

———. "The Ruins of Representation: Shadow Survivance and the Literature of Dominance." *An Other Tongue: Nation and Ethnicity in the Linguistic Borderlands.* Ed. Alfred Arteaga. Durham: Duke UP, 1994. 139–167. Print.

Weinstock, Jeffrey Andrew. "Ten Minutes for Seven Letters: Reading *Beloved*'s Epitaph." *The Arizona Quarterly* 61.3 (2005): 129–152. Print.

Whitehead, Anne. *Trauma Fiction.* Edinburgh: Edinburgh UP, 2004. Print.

Wideman, Jon Edgar. "The Healing of Velma Henry." Rev. of *The Salt Eaters* by Toni Cade Bambara. *New York Times Book Review* 1 June 1980. 14+. Print.

Williams, John. *Fiction as False Document: The Reception of E. L. Doctorow in the Postmodern Age.* Columbia, SC: Camden House, 1996. Print.

Winsbro, Bonnie. *Supernatural Forces: Belief, Difference, and Power in Contemporary Works by Ethnic Women.* Amherst: U of Massachusetts P, 1993. Print.

Wolfe, Tom. *The Bonfire of the Vanities.* New York: Farrar, Straus, 1987. Print.

Zamora, Lois Parkinson. "Magical Romance/Magical Realism: Ghosts in U.S. and Latin American Fiction." *Magical Realism: Theory, History, Community.* Ed. Lois Parkinson Zamora and Wendy B. Faris. Durham: Duke UP, 1995. Print.

Index